IN THE [illegible]

The police force which serves the Lords of the Exchange is known as the Regulators. Crack men. Tough, lean, brutal. And the toughest and finest was—*was*—the melancholy fighter with the strange, haunted golden eyes that made him a legend before his fall.

He is a member of the house and lineage of Dragonard, so his name is also Dragonard.

Dragonard the murderer.
Dragonard the madman.
Dragonard the beast.

This is his adventure.

JOHN JAKES

WHEN THE STAR KINGS DIE

ace books
A Division of Charter Communications Inc.
A GROSSET & DUNLAP COMPANY
1120 Avenue of the Americas
New York, New York 10036

WHEN THE STAR KINGS DIE

An ACE Book

Cover art by *Alex Ebel*

First Ace printing: October 1967
Second Ace printing: March 1978

Printed in U.S.A.

This is for

JACK and PHOEBE GAUGHAN

PROLOGUE

SEE, THEN, II GALAXY.

It wheels and a billion stars wheel with it, far in space from the First Home, the Earth, far in future time from the first Out-riding in the lightships, that now-ancient history which carried man out past the point of returning, to where he could become, without aid from the First Home, the master of II Galaxy.

In II Galaxy, savagery and opulence live side by side in an uneasy tension on planet after planet. Common people of all the star races, Terran and otherwise, grub out existence in near primitive surroundings, ruled by the loose confederation of ageless, deathless star kings—

The Lords of the Exchange.

Ten thousand years before this moment, a series of devastating planetary wars wracked II Galaxy. Before the wars, power was concentrated in the great houses, the great commercial corporations which had existed and expanded and extended their dominion since the primitive days of folk-memory, the time of the Out-riding from the First Home.

When the devastations guttered out, leaving planets dead or burning by the hundreds and the thousands, the commercial corporations lived on in the wreckage. But they rose with new bodies, like phoenixes.

Each house, each corporation, became a centralized bloc of political power operated by survivors who were not necessarily scrupulous. And thus came gradual collusion to control the flow of essential commodities. Thus also came intermarriage and interbreeding, a thinning and rottening of the corporate blood.

And at the end of centuries the rulers of the houses joined as the star kings in loose but dominant alliance, their aim not to rule for the good of all, but to rule for ruling's sake, and to preserve their houses.

These are the Lords of the Exchange, hereditary tyrants like Easkod X and Genmo II, Arsgrat the Golden, Xero II and Stanbrans and Unilev and Mishubi—star kings all, each ruling a few worlds ruthlessly, each with a corrupted name echoing that of the corporation his ruthless forbears seized at the end of the devastating galactic wars ten thousand years ago.

The police force which serves the Lords of the Exchange is known as the Regulators. Crack men. Tough, lean, brutal. And the toughest and finest was—*was*—the melancholy fighter with the strange, haunted golden eyes that made him a legend before his fall.

He is a member of the house and lineage of Dragonard, so his name is also Dragonard.

Dragonard the murderer.

Dragonard the madman.

Dragonard the beast.

This is his adventure, in the tenth age of the star kings of II Galaxy.

1

ON THE PRISON PLANET, electronic locks released once a day in the late afternoon. Today's time was coming soon.

Dragonard knew exactly how many times the locks had released since his own Regulators had brought him sky-sledding here, none of them willing to look him directly in the eye.

He'd heard the low humming, then the cold click 738 times.

Two years was enough. He listened to the lock now, thinking, *Enough. What's ahead but rotting here the rest of my days?*

It didn't matter greatly that their chances were perilously small. Nor did it matter that those plotting were the worst of the several thousand incorrigibles within Fortress Rankor, the only human establishment on the scarred and lifeless planet whirling at the rim of II Galaxy.

The door unlocked and Dragonard rose from the bed where he'd been sprawled. He stretched his long arms. Then he walked across the small, brightly illuminated chamber whose walls were of foamed steel. He pushed at the door, pushed through. His mind clicked the commitment.

I'll go. I'll try with them.

He felt better, even though the decision sharpened his senses with all the raw awareness of the peril ahead.

The compound of Fortress Rankor was huge, three times the size of a regulation spacefield. Great red modified-laser lanterns shed light on it from the surrounding high walls where guards stood at attention every ten yards. From tiers of cells on the two inner sides of the compound, hundreds of men, white, black, green, yellow, shuffled forth and down iron staircases, to shuffle in larger crowds on the cold stone of the compound floor.

Maxmillion Dragonard did not speak to the men who came from the cells on either side of him. He joined the queue at the stairs, walked down in silence. He hated his gray tunic, breeches, prison boots. As he reached the compound floor he looked around. Men pushing up behind automatically walked wide of him on either side, mumbling among themselves, saying nothing to him. The legend lingered. Men smelled danger, destruction when they came too near the tall man whose electronic code name had been MAXDRAGON.

To the right, under the wall, Dragonard saw the seven plotters talking and he walked that way. The compound smelled sulphurous, like all of Rankor. The gray fog seldom lifted. It eddied and whirled now, drifting in from the rock moors beyond the walls. Under the laser light, prisoners standing and staring at nothing but their own hopelessness became reddish phantoms, half-seen even at close range in the chill murk.

The plotters stopped talking as Dragonard approached. Of the seven, two were uniped Solarians, fur-faced and tusked. Two were pale pink Varloids, constantly emitting a high, thin vibration from their antennae. Dragonard picked this up, noting the slight change in frequency that indicated tension. The other three were of Terran descent, the biggest being Tingo Spellhands. He had the place of respect, a section of wall against which to lean.

Tingo Spellhands had dark wavy hair, a long jaw and a rather crooked mouth which always seemed to be smiling; Spellhands had no humor in him, though. Below the cuffs of his tunic hung dull silver hands, free of rust, beautifully articulated. Each fingertip was clear crystal back to the first joint. The crystals were dark.

Though Spellhands stood tall, Dragonard stood taller. Because of his considerable height, he tended to stoop. His mouth and jaw were strong. His strange gold eyes were very direct: lawbreakers used to scream when the man with the golden eyes caught them. Even now, with Dragonard simply standing at the edge of the group, those eyes commanded silence. Dragonard had a melancholy look to him, the melancholy of the starwolf, the single hunter without mercy.

On the last finger of his right hand he wore a gold ring with an oval black stone. The stone's long dimension paralleled the bone of his finger. Into the black stone were etched images of two mythical beasts, a snarling lion and a rising phoenix, the sign of the house of Dragonard. Of all his personal possessions, only the ring had not been confiscated by prison authorities.

"Take it your presence indicates a yes, Commander?" Spellhands asked.

"Let's drop the 'Commander.' I've said that before."

Tingo Spellhands never stopped smiling. "Yes, I do forget that you aren't the big policeman any longer. Just a killer like most of the rest of us."

The corner of Dragonard's mouth ticked. Spellhands roused red wrath in him. "And you, of course, were the most honorable of men before they caught you. A slaver who didn't even mind snatching children as long as they had esper talents you could sell."

Tingo Spellhands flexed the metal hands. "Is it going to be an insult match?"

"That's according to how you feel, slaver. You started the 'Commander' business."

"Pretty high and mighty for a cashiered Regulator," one of the other Terrans grumbled.

Dragonard turned. The red light washed like a tide in his mind. His throat dried up.

No. *Control. Control!*

He fought for it, gained it.

He swallowed and returned his big, thin-fingered hands to his pockets.

The beginnings of the berserk seizures hadn't bothered him much on Rankor. Probably this was because none of these men was worth the rage he used to feel when he captured a particularly scrofulous criminal. In those days, rage triggered whatever bad, tortured relays were in his mind that set off the neurological fits. He hadn't had a full seizure since the one that sent him here, and he didn't intend to have one because of Spellhands.

"All right," Spellhands said to the Terran who'd grumbled. It was sufficient; the man shut up. "You in, then, Dragonard?"

"I am. Why you invited me is another question."

Spellhands chuckled. "When you want to add a killing machine to the team, add the best. We—"

Abruptly the ex-slaver lifted his right hand and stared at the dark crystal fingertips. A pair of guards passed. Two of the Solarians clicked their tusks in coversational code. The guards gave the group a long stare, then drifted on. They clutched their ray rifles tightly with mittened hands.

Nearly three dozen guard teams in all mingled among the massed prisoners. There had been riots on Rankor before, near massacres. Dragonard caught the glance of one of the guards looking back at them. A young one, barely out of the Civil Servant Academy. The guard had recognized him. Dragonard knew.

The gold eyes always gave it away. *Maxdragon? Yes, he's the one.* It was a bitter satisfaction.

Dragonard felt a tug at his sleeve. Spellhands said softly, "Notice that one?"

"The youngster? What about him?"

"Two hundred of them rotated in last night. That means two hundred veterans gone."

A frown scarred Dragonard's forehead. "That's at least a week ahead of schedule."

One of the Solarians clicked his tusks, then said in a broken version of the Common Tongue, "The older veterans were required immediately, our informants tell us, for strike duty at another location."

"Which means that our timetable can move ahead," Spellhands said. "We weren't going to go until the regular rotation brought the kids in." Seeing Dragonard's doubt, Spellhands added, "Listen, my sources are reliable."

"I believe that. You'd kill any ones who weren't."

"At least we understand each other." Spellhands glanced both ways. No guards were near. The fog drifted. The laser light washed eerily over the hundreds and hundreds of standing men. "We won't get another green crop of guards for a six-month. You just accepted the bid to the dance in time, Comman—uh, Dragonard. I've had the key to the skysled pool for three weeks. I have only one time scrambler."

"For unlocking one cell door." Dragonard nodded. "I won't ask you where it came from."

"Work every day in the modulation ship, I," chittered the Varloid on Dragonard's left.

All right, that explains it. Who uses the scrambler?" he asked.

"Why, we were just coming to that."

Spellhands reached into his tunic pocket with his

right hand. He drew his hand out, cupped shut. He shook it. There was a multiple clicking.

"The man who uses the time scrambler will have the roughest row to plow. He'll have to open his own door, take out the tier guard, then go to the electro-armory and bring back a universal power cell for these." Spellhands raised his hands. On the backplate of the left one Dragonard saw a small, square, hinged panel. "With the power cell inside my left hand, the fingers'll light up like yule trees. Then taking out the rest of the guards'll be easy. I paid a pretty credit for these hands a long time ago. Mine were cut off in an accident when—but you don't want biography. You don't give a damn where I came from, do you, Dragonard? All you want is out of this hole, and off Rankor in a skysled, am I right?"

Slowly Dragonard said, "That's right. You don't like me; I don't like you. We might as well let it lie that way. Stick to business and we'll all get where we want."

"With luck," Spellhands agreed. "With some luck and guts. As soon as my hands are powered, the finger lights will hypno any guard who looks at 'em. The man who fetches the power cell will have to find a blaster too. He'll slice me out of the cell so I can power up. But from then on, it's smooth. Right to the skysled pool and off. Right now we have to decide who takes the first leg, who goes out of his cell and to the armory." Spellhands shook his hand again, the clicking a little louder. "In here are pebbles."

Dragonard's gold eyes lidded. "How many?"

"Eight. We figured you couldn't stand Rankor much longer, and that you'd be in."

Damnably right, Dragonard thought, hating the man for knowing. A little reddish flicker stirred at the edge of his mind. He fought it back, damped it.

"One of the pebbles has a cross scratched on it. That man goes," Spellhands said.

"Start the drawing," Dragonard said.

Tingo Spellhands held his hand behind his back. A Solarian acted as lookout, his back turned toward the group. Click-clack went the tusks.

"All is cleared, no guard pairs close by. Draw, you."

The other Solarian reached behind Spellhands swiftly. He opened his palm to display an unmarked pebble. He dropped it, covered it with his single clawed footpad; the Solarians wore no boots.

The bulb-bellied little Terran with the moustache drew next. A blank. He tucked the pebble in his belt.

Through the compound rumbled the single voice that was a thousand more voices, a hopeless mumble of hopeless men. The laser lights shone in the drifting fog. On the stone parapets the guards at parade-rest never took their eyes off the milling men below.

Dragonard stood with his hands in his pockets. He hated the idea of escape like this, but he'd hate himself more if he stayed on Rankor the rest of his years. His sentence was lifetime. He was more than merely dangerous to the galactic society of the Lords of the Exchange; he was a Regulator gone bad. And a high Regulator, which was even worse. It had made the sentence heavier.

They had very little chance to escape, Dragonard knew. But being slaughtered by blasters or ray rifles might be a boon.

"You draw next," said Spellhands to Dragonard.

The tall man with the gold eyes reached around the ex-slaver. He felt the man's hand twist slightly, angle his palm so that one side was higher than another. The pebbles rolled. Dragonard picked one blind and drew it out.

Another pair of guards approached. When they'd passed on, Dragonard extended his hand, uncurled the fingers. Without looking, he knew what he would see.

There was a curt laugh from Spellhands. "The game's all over."

Dragonard felt the cross scratched into the pebble's surface and ground the stone under his heel without glancing at it. He knew Spellhands had manipulated the pebbles, using a sleight to guarantee that Dragonard drew the cross and the riskiest part of the escape plan.

Curiously, that agreed with Dragonard. To move, to act, no matter how dangerously, would come as a relief. He felt his frustration sloughing off. On the parapets the guard was changing; before many more moments the amplified horns would bleat the end of the exercise period.

"Give me the time scrambler," Dragonard said.

"You don't seem upset that you drew the rough part," Spellhands said.

"I'm not, since you wanted me to have it. Don't you trust yourself?"

The ex-slaver's neck reddened. "Bast—" he began between his teeth.

"Come on, I'll take it." Dragonard's long fingers wiggled.

"Not in plain sight, you damn fool. I'll bump against you when we file back in. Slip it into your pocket."

Spellhands was glaring. Instinctive dislike had leaped like lightning between the two men from their first meeting months ago in the prison foodhall. Dragonard had accepted this, never stopping to wonder why. Now the ex-slaver's hatred was so shiningly naked in his eyes that Dragonard did wonder at last.

Spellhands barely kept his smile in place as he began: "Some general instructions. First, wait till the midnight watch-mark is over, then go. Take out the guard in your tier plus any of the other guards you run into in the electro-armory. Make sure that you take them out all the way. Kill them."

Dragonard's right brow went up like a hook. Then it flattened out. "I'll do it my way."

"You'll kill them," Spellhands repeated under his breath. "Then we'll be certain."

"You're not going to tell me who to kill, Tingo my friend," said Dragonard quietly.

Spellhands' mouth screwed up. "Squeamish? I don't believe it. Your guts didn't run yellow when you killed your prisoners. Oh, I've heard how you did it. Went berserk, foamed at the mouth, beat them—"

Now Dragonard's gold eyes could barely be seen under his lids. "Be careful."

"Has life got so precious to you all of a sudden?" Spellhands blustered on. "Or maybe it's this way—maybe those other times you had helpers, Regulators who held the poor sons of bitches kicking and screaming while you beat them—"

The red light burst in Dragonard's mind. Hands up, he went for the throat.

Gagging, flailing, Spellhands slammed against the wall. He jabbed fingers at Dragonard's eyes. Dragonard shook him like a doll. He could feel himself beginning to shudder with violence. His fingers constricted.

Spellhands kicked at his groin hard, hurting him. On the parapet one of the guards rang his portable alarm, *gong, gong, gong, gong*. Teams in the yard converged. The Varloids tried to pull the struggling men apart, their vibrations keening a high soprano that hurt Dragonard's ears.

In his brain the red mist washed, lapped, swallowed sense. He felt the exultation of killing.

The Varloids pried his hands from Spellhands' throat and Dragonard collapsed against his foe.

Sense returned as the redness waned. Horror ate his vitals, the horror of borderline moments he had experienced before, moments in which a part of him that was neurologically broken down took over, demanding someone's death, while the real, sane part of him figuratively stood away, sick and powerless to handle the monster that he had become.

His temples hurt. Guard boots thrummed closer.

"All right, all right, you scum! Break it up or we'll give you a stun beam!"

Dragonard's hands seemed to get caught in the

folds of Spellhands' tunic as he pushed off, then stood up. He dropped his hands into his pockets. His eyes looked luminous.

"You hate me too much, Spellhands. I don't understand why."

Spellhands rubbed his throat. "The stink of the law's still on you, prison or not."

"It's the Regulators you hate."

"It's you, you bastard, because you're the closest one, and the snottiest—"

The guards thrust in. The Solarians had sensed the danger to the escape plan and had interposed themselves between the fighting Terrans and the guards, feigning clumsiness. There were a few seconds in which Dragonard and Spellhands still leaned close together, snarling.

"You're out, Commander. You're out of the hand and the game." Spellhands cracked a vicious smile. "I'm going to report to the guards that you—"

"Report nothing." Dragonard patted his pocket. "When I brushed against you, I picked the time scrambler out of your pocket. Feel if you don't believe me."

Astonished, Spellhands did just that. His face congealed with hate again, then with a kind of disgusted envy. Spellhands understood that Dragonard had outguessed him, had gone one mental leap ahead and estimated that Spellhands might turn on him and turn him in, and so had stolen the key to freedom as insurance.

Dragonard's fingers touched the cool metal capsule in his pocket as the guards finally thrust them apart. The guards used their ring cameras to photo the two prisoners.

"Both of you will come up for disciplinary exam tomorrow," the head guard cracked. "Fighting is a minimum of ten penance credits."

"So that's news," Spellhands said. He never took his eyes from Dragonard.

From the radar castles at the corners of the high walls the amplified horns roared, *OWgah, OWgah, OWgah, OWgah*. Men stirred, shuffling toward the stairs, and the guards withdrew. The Varloids and the Solarians grouped around Spellhands and his two Terran friends. Dragonard stood alone.

But he had the time scrambler safe.

Guards jog-trotted past, shouting at the prisoners to move along to the stairs and up to the tiers. Again Dragonard noted the youthfulness of the new replacements.

The prison garrison would never be greener than now. In a week, the young troops in on rotation would be accepting bribes and stomping inmates for amusement like old hands.

Dragonard liked the feeling of events accelerating as he started for the stairs to his tier, then turned and walked back to Spellhands.

"Some of your ideas aren't bad, Tingo my friend. Such as acting swiftly. Be ready after the midnight watch-mark." Speaking it, Dragonard was committed. "I say we go tonight."

A guard moved in to prod him with a ray rifle. Laughing, Dragonard joined the shuffling lines of men.

II

THE NIGHT HOURS dragged. Bells chimed the hourly watch-marks. Dragonard paced his cell.

The food service tube, located in one wall near the floor next to the waste service tube, delivered his evening meal. He flushed the food down the waste tube, returning the utensils empty to the food service tube. He couldn't stomach anything tonight. But an uneaten meal, returned, checked and noted, might result in a night call by one of the prison doctors. Better to be cautious.

At one point Dragonard threw his head back and laughed hard. He was acting as though they had a chance!

Still, inaction, indecision could be a death too. And he would never have a reprieve from the Lords of the Exchange.

When he had desperately wanted aid for his condition, his request had been denied with the statement that the techniques for repairing his mental difficulties, the strange, lethal short circuits in his mind, were nonexistent. Those techniques, he was informed, had been lost along with a vast body of human knowledge in the radiation litter of the planet wars ten centuries ago.

This information had come down directly from the assembled Lords. Dragonard's superior, a Sectioner, had bucked the desperate appeal for help directly up to them. Good old Valk. Of all the Regulators, only Dragonard's commandant had stood by him during the first complicated petition to the authorities, and again two years ago, when the actual killing took place. Even the High Commander of the Regulators, a man Dragonard had seen only once during a review on a parade field, had scrupulously avoided dealing with the request for help and the subsequent charge of murder.

Well, he'd been over that ground mentally a thousand times. There was no cure in known neurotechnology for the apparent birth defect which produced his periods of intense hostility and insane rage. It was no one's fault, he supposed, that he was cripple-minded. Most times, though—as for instance now—he felt as though the malady were imaginary, as though it could not possibly exist.

But in those other times, like when he'd gone for the throat of Spellhands, he couldn't stop it.

And tonight everything would have to be cool, orderly, cautious. Dragonard's palms sweated.

The midnight watch-mark chimed. On schedule, the cell lights blinked out. Dragonard sucked in a breath. He dropped to his knees beside the door.

Carefully he pulled out the time scrambler. In two years of prison, his fingers hadn't forgotten how to operate one. He set the calibrations, then he applied the anti-molecular face to the door, near the electronic lock. He held the scrambler in place for five seconds after punching in the stub trigger.

Then he let go. No clatter disturbed the dark. The scrambler held fast.

The cell ventilators whispered. Above their hum he heard another low sound, spark-like. The anti-m face of the scrambler had fused with the door metal. In another minute or two—

From somewhere inside the door's heart came a ratchet noise. It repeated.

Dragonard pried at the door's edge and it swung in toward him. He blocked it with his knee, listening.

Booted feet walked the tier, coming closer. Dragonard stood, eased the door all the way open, and waited in the solid dark of the opening. The moor-mist of Rankor blowing over the walls smelled sweet as honey, free as the freshest wind.

The compound was dark: all the laser lights had been turned off. Guards stalked the parapets between the dim radar castles at the tower corners. A night mail skysled burned across the sky, leaving a yellow trail for the fog to close over.

The pit of Dragonard's belly hurt. The guard appeared outside the door, facing straight ahead. Dragonard didn't give him the benefit of a warning. He jumped.

Slapping his hand over the guard's mouth. Dragonard threw the man to the concrete. His old training came back. His stiffened fingers jabbed the base of the man's throat.

The guard coughed, rolled over against the outer

rail. Dragonard dragged him inside the cell. He put on the uniform blouse which was too snug, and the billed cap, which fitted. He slipped the guard's blaster into his belt. Then he went out, closed the cell door and walked to his right.

Sweat congealed at the fringes of his sideburns, trickling down his cheeks even though the night was cool.

Ahead, a single lamp burned over the entrance to the gravtube at the end of the tier. A guard stood at attention beside the tube, a green recruit in a fresh-pressed outfit. Dragonard speeded up his walk. He touched his cap bill as he went right by, stepping into the down gravtube and starting down at the controlled rate with nothing under him but force.

"Salute," the guard said as Dragonard dropped out of sight. Then a yell: "Hold on! What color pants are those you—?"

"Gray," Dragonard breathed, shooting the blaster up the tube.

The stun charge flung the guard back out of sight. Dragonard examined the weapon. Worse luck, it had a max stun limit of nine minutes. Should he have switched over? Spellhands had wanted him to kill.

He couldn't do it though. Not even if a battalion of guards recognized that he was wearing prisoner's pants under the uniform top.

He descended to the second sub-level and stepped off. No guards at all were in this dimly lighted length of corridor. He passed the nutritional lab, the offices of the socioadjustment staff, and he flattened against the left wall at an L-junction.

He'd read every card in the prison library, including the elaborate Propaganda Ministry brochure covering Rankor's facilities. He had memorized every floor plan too, in the event someone, someday, might want to try a breakout. At last Spellhands had approached. The laborious memorization paid off.

Dragonard looked around the corner of the wall. Two guards lounged in a waist-high booth at the large double doors of the electro-armory. Dragonard sighted and triggered.

The first guard sprawled, coughing. The second grabbed for his piece. Dragonard's charge caught him in mid-grab. The guard folded down across the booth's control console.

As the guard fell, Dragonard was running. Dragged down by the dead weight of his own inert body, the guard's hand clawed across console switches. One set of switches saved Dragonard time by opening the double doors and flashing on the interior lights.

Another switch sprang the alarms. The corridor howled with ear-hurting sirens.

"Blown it!" Dragonard snarled, diving into the electro-armory and down the aisles between the conveyor bins.

He located the bins of universal power cells, stuffed three of the small, round gray discs into the pockets of his uniform blouse, and snatched a gas rifle as he ran out.

Yelling guards poured at him from the right. Dragonard butted the rifle against his hip and hit the continuous spray bar. From the fan nozzle bluish gas gouted, filling the corridor wall to wall.

Dragonard backed up steadily, quit firing as he rounded the corner again and bolted for the grav-tubes. One drugged guard managed to stagger through the fumes and aim his blaster. Dragonard went into the up tube as the beam melted the floor tile at the tube's entrance.

He reached the tier above his own, Spellhands' tier, swiftly. Three more guards were approaching on the double. A blaster switched on to full cut loose and Dragonard backed quickly away from the spurting fire that ate up the concrete near his boots. He let them have the next gas rifle cylinder full force.

Because the tier was open on one side, the effect of the gas was somewhat weakened: the guards staggered against each other as though suffering a good case of intoxication. Dragonard clipped one in the jaw with the butt of the gas rifle, and bowled past the other two. A blaster beam hissed near his shoulder. He zigzagged, threw the gas rifle away, spun. Flat against the wall with his teeth peeled back and his gold eyes bright, he stunned one of the two behind him, then the other.

All the laser lights in the compound flashed on. The radar castles lit up, gun ports fell away, and powerful cannon nosed out and began sweeping the compound in silent arcs. Dragonard counted cell doors, read nameplates. He came to one whose plate read SPELLHANDS / 15 - 25.

Dragonard backed against the rail, not bothering to shout and warn Spellhands inside. There was warning noise enough. Guards poured out of the gravtubes. The tier concrete puddled and smoked and burned all around his feet.

He fired down at a sharp angle. The blaster beam cut the electronic lock to junk. He pulled at the door and dived inside into the darkness where Spellhands breathed heavily.

"Got three."

"And set all the alarms off too. Nice work."

"Couldn't be helped. Where's your damn hand? Get the plate open."

The only illumination in the cell came from the crisscross of blaster beams sputtering by outside. Guards shouted, forming into attack groups. Dragonard fumbled to find Spellhands' left hand in the dark. With the fingertips of his free hand, Dragonard located the opening in the back of the metal hand and snapped up the spring cover plate. He thrust one of the universal cells down into the circular receptacle.

A spang of closing metal. Spellhands lunged by, laughing.

"Watch your eyes, Commander."

The crystal ends of his ten fingers burst into wild, prismatic brilliance. The light's backwash drove darts of pain into Dragonard's eyeballs. He flung his forearm across his nose for a shield.

Spellhands was outside, on the cement tier. One hand pointed to the left, the other to the right. He wriggled his fingers like a sideshow mesmerist. From those crystal tips radiated faintly visible waves of light, burning into Dragonard's mind like hallucinations, optical echoes.

The light in the crystal fingertips constantly

changed color, running through the spectrum and back again in split seconds. The guards running from both left and right went down.

A ray cannon in one of the radar castles on the far wall opened up. Greenish light sizzled at them. Dragonard hit Spellhands with his shoulder, driving him out of the way as the cannon sawed a fuming hole through the thick cellblock wall.

"Thanks, Commander," Spellhands choked, stumbling up off his knees. "Blast the next two cells down from mine. Those are the Solarians."

A quick beam shot at each electronic lock had the unipeds free in a moment. The cannon fired again. Thunder smote the foggy night and a ten foot hole appeared in the cellblock wall. The tier floor above creaked, swayed, then buckled in a shower of cement dust. A guard clinging to the rail up there lost his balance and fell shrieking to smash to blood on the compound floor.

Spellhands threw the switch on the back of his right hand, shutting off both. He led Dragonard and the Solarians to the gravtubes. The Solarians clicked their tusks; slobber dripped from their wet black snouts.

"Where are your Varloids and your Terran friends?" Dragonard shouted as they jumped over the clot of fallen guards. Mesmerized by the powerful optical rays in the mechanical hands, they sprawled with contented faces. A couple of them actually smiled.

"Next level above." Spellhands headed into the down gravtube.

Dragonard pulled on his arm. The sirens howled. "The up tube's over here."

Spellhands shook his head. "Let the Varloids stay. I don't owe them a damn thing and we can't afford time with the whole fortress awake."

"You don't owe them anything except a promise—"

Tingo Spellhands jerked his head forward in a kind of silent, contemptuous spitting motion. "You want to argue ethics, Commander? Or do you want to follow me and my little key to the skysled pool and hope we can still get out of here?"

The cannon on the radar castle flamed green and a puffball of smoke and thunder rocked the tier just a few feet from them. The Solarians jumped into the gravtube after Spellhands. Dragonard followed them down, his hand gripped tightly around his blaster, his gold eyes ugly.

III

AT THE main level Spellhands jumped out and switched his fingers on. Dragonard and the furry Solarians crowded after him as Spellhands cut the corridor ahead with swatches of fluctuating light.

By turning his head forty-five degrees to the side and squinting, Dragonard could still see where he was going. The backwash of brilliance produced only a bearable, throbbing pain that way.

A clutch of armed guards blocked the load zone, a concrete esplanade alongside several moving belt-ways that ran parallel for a short distance before branching off down tunnels. Spellhands lit up, knocked the guards out to a man, then snapped his hands dark again.

"Go over to the third belt," he ordered. "It's high speed, straight to the skysled pool."

Voices rattled off the walls of the bright corridor behind and Dragonard swung around. Two more guards appeared. One, with a ray rifle, dropped to his knees for a steady aim. Spellhands was already leaping across the first and second belts. The first Solarian hopped after him on his single limb.

Dragonard cursed, fumbling with the adjustment which loaded a new stun charge into his blaster. Those seconds cost him. The guard fired.

The second Solarian let out a moan and smashed forward, a lethal hole burned through the prison tunic into the furred back. The Solarian's lower limb slipped down between the second and third belts. As his whole lower body was sucked into the machinery, the Solarian squealed in mortal pain.

Dragonard fired two stun charges; the guards dropped. The first Solarian was struggling to pull his companion's body out of the gearworks under the belts. Already the second belt had slowed down. The third buckled, folding up on itself in several places.

The harder the Solarian pulled, the louder the caught one squealed. The stench of burned fur and leaking life fluid mingled nauseously in the air.

Dragonard jumped the first belt, landed on the second, and bent down to pull.

"That one's done for!" Spellhands shouted. "Leave him!"

"There's a chance we can—"

Spellhands caught Dragonard's shoulder and pulled savagely, Dragonard spilled onto the third, buckling belt. Spellhands tore the blaster from his hand.

"Dammit, I'm running this!"

Crouching at the edge of the third belt, Spellhands shoved the blaster down against the Solarian's trunk. The creature was sunk to its waist in the grinding, clattering machinery. The Solarian recognized death: its sea-green pupils grew huge, filling all of its eyesockets.

Spellhands fired, using the blaster as a slicing tool. He cut the Solarian in half at the waist.

Smoke roiled and the fur stench dug into Dragonard's pores. He regained his feet, shaking with horror, disbelief, rage. The caught Solarian mewed and clicked its tusks once as it died.

Spellhands seized the creature's head-hair and heaved. The head, trunk and arms separated, burned away from the lower body. Brown anise-scented life fluid leaked all over the belts as Spellhands threw the remains back onto the esplanade. Then he sharpened the blaster beam to a needle and fired a few bursts between the belt edges.

Red sparks shot up, then subsided. With a wrench and jolt the third belt unbuckled and picked up speed.

The remaining Solarian watched Spellhands closely. It emitted its hate scent, but Spellhands had the blaster. Dragonard rode the speeding belt wide-legged, his feelings plain on his face. Spellhands wiped a brown drop from his cheek.

"Did I injure your tender sensibilities, Commander?" he asked.

"Give me the blaster," Dragonard said.

Spellhands seemed to debate it silently; then he tossed the weapon. Dragonard caught it.

"I ask you again," Spellhands said. "What do you want? Charity or escape?"

Dragonard's gold eyes slitted down. The wind rushed at his back as the belt inclined downward. "It's a nasty choice, you bastard."

"But a bastard who's engineering what looks like a successful escape. *Watch your head!*"

His cry spun Dragonard around. The keystone arch of a tunnel rushed and loomed. Dragonard's body obeyed what wasn't even a consciously-worded thought. He dropped on his face.

The belt sped them into the dark. Another second standing and he'd have been decapitated.

Somewhere in the rushing blackness, Spellhands breathed. The belt gears sang back on pitch now and Dragonard climbed to his knees. Light bloomed ahead. Spellhands touched Dragonard's sleeve with his crystal fingers.

"That's the skysled pool station. All off that're going off."

Dragonard pulled away. "Put your hands on me one more time and I'll kill you."

Spellhands heard how serious he was, and drew back with an obscene snort. The Solarian hovered near as the belt carried him into the light. Dragonard sprang onto the concrete and then he gave the Solarian a helping hand; Spellhands made the leap by himself.

Sirens wailed from amplifiers set in the ceiling of the deserted, brightly lighted concrete platform. Spellhands bobbed his head. The other two followed him toward the sole exit from the platform, a ponderous-looking metal door.

From his tunic Spellhands pulled a small metal cube. He triggered it, then pressed it in place on the door.

The pool door key had to be held in place for sixty-five seconds. Dragonard shoved his hair back out of his eyes. The Solarian's tusks clicked faintly.

Behind them the belts rumbled along and voices rose above the machinery murmur. A search party, riding the belt in pursuit—

A faint interlocking of gears came from the door. Spellhands jerked the little cube of a key back, and threw it toward the belt moving past the esplanade. "Made it to destruct in case I got caught with it," he said as the cube dropped onto the belt and exploded.

Smoke puffed up and the belt ripped in half. The end shoving in from the way they'd come began to fold up in huge, rug-like loops. Dragonard grudgingly admitted to himself that Spellhands covered the details. Oaths, shouts told him the pursuit party had been jerked to a halt in the tunnel.

Foggy air washed over his face as he followed Spellhands and the Solarian through the door into a small square compound open to the misty night sky.

Prison skysleds stood in two neat rows, berthed on their rockers. In the snout of each an iron ring had been fused; a chain ran along through the rings, fixed to steel uprights at either end. Spellhands told Dragonard to cut one of the chains. Guards appeared from the single small radar castle at the junction of two walls.

While Dragonard fired away at the chain with the blaster, Spellhands lit his fingers. The distance to the wall was considerable so it took long seconds for the half-seen, half-sensed waves of light to reach. One of the guards raced to a laser lantern, swung it in its swivel mount and flooded the compound with red radiance, all before he went to sleep on his feet and then crumpled. Two ray rifles fired from the castle, a bolt apiece. Then their operators went out too.

Dragonard hauled the cut chain out of the rings of half a dozen skysleds. Spellhands laughed out loud now. He levered up the bubble of a four-man sled.

"Don't look so glum, Commander. It's been cake this far, hasn't it?"

"Bloody cake. Get in and let's get the hell out of here."

Spellhands threw a leg over the hatch lip. That was when the lights came out of the dark.

They came straight and steady, bright beams crisscrossing down from overhead. Dragonard recognized the spitting whoosh of larger skysleds. In a moment their jet trails appeared like fingers of fire in the murk above. Next Dragonard recognized the configuration of the first ship to drop below the ceiling with its fore-lantern lighting up the compound.

"Those are Regulator sleds!"

Head twisted around, Spellhands stared, not believing. The truth registered as a second skysled dropped into sight, then a third. Three more followed.

They held on retros, all of their fore-lanterns probing down to make the compound shine as white as day.

Inside the command blips, helmeted heads were black against winking consoles. The first of the skysleds peeled off, its burners sputtering. It skimmed down above the center of the compound. Men inside pointed, gestured. The hatchway fell open as the skysled decelerated and hovered.

Tingo Spellhands howled his anger: "How did they get there? How!"

"Shut up and get in the sled." Dragonard's stomach was frozen. They were trapped.

Spellhands fumbled at the switch for his fingers. He stared hard into Dragonard's gold eyes. His mouth convulsed.

"You. It was *you* who sold us out."

"You're crazy. I want out of here as badly—"

"Oh no, I can see how you thought: tip off the Regulators about the break, earn yourself some freedom credits—"

Spellhands snapped the hand switch. Light smote Dragonard in the eyeballs like fire. He threw himself backwards onto the ground, away.

As he fell he had distorted, surrealistic view of an alloy ladder tumbling down out of the skysled hatch, and four uniformed Regulators coming down the ladder swiftly. Dragonard's head struck ground, muffling a cry from the skysled hatch: ". . . The one we want. Don't let—"

Kicking, rolling, Dragonard rolled under a sled's snout to get away from the blazing lights that poured from Spellhands' fingers. The ex-slaver dodged around and under the ring snout. Dragonard rolled again, but Spellhands was quicker. The hypnotic lights caught him full in the eyes. He was half on his feet. He fell over again, stunned. His muscles stretched out, turning viscous, fast emptying of power to move him.

"Get that crazy man away from him and fast!" a voice bawled from the hovering sled. Rolling again, Dragonard thought he ought to recognize the voice, but he couldn't. Spellhands came on, using his hands like fans back and forth through the air.

Dragonard banged against the next sled in line. He got up and jumped head first over the bubble and slid down the other side with the wind knocked out of him.

The dancing, scintillant waves of light bent under the sled's nose. They made his head beat with pain—

The night turned into chaos.

Voices clamored and boots rang down hard. Spellhands screamed his obscenities at the top of his lungs as he hunted after Dragonard.

Breathing violently, Dragonard realized that the hypnotic light had diminished and he stood up behind the skysled. Spellhands realized that capture was close and he bolted down the aisle between the two ranks of docked sleds. A Regulator called for him to halt. The laser light and the lanterns from the hovering sleds made the Regulator's war helmet with its lightning-jag insignia shine like a skull.

Spellhands swung around in his tracks, lighted hands blazing. Behind them his face was a sweaty mask, the eyes screwed down to slits so that backglare wouldn't affect him. The Regulator was young, supple, fast. He dragged his blaster loose from the holster and aimed for Spellhands' left leg and fired.

The slaver screamed and pitched backward. From his left knee down, nothing was left. His kneecap had become a tatter of cartilage and torn prison-gray cloth and fused flesh. It smoked like a charred stick. He flopped back and forth like an animal.

The Regulators moved into a tight half-circle.

Dragonard hid behind one of the skysleds, confused.

The Regulators had shot Spellhands with the cold efficiency of professional police dealing with a vicious criminal. But now Spellhands lay forgotten. The ex-slaver propped himself on an elbow, howling.

"Commander—you—Commander! As long—as I breathe—I'm going to hunt you—make you pay. . . . Nobody—sells Tingo Spellhands out. . . . *I'm crippled!"* The scream rose. *"I'm crippled . . .!"* And dissolved into the incoherent bay of an animal.

The Regulators advanced cautiously toward where Dragonard hid, paying no attention to the Solarian either. Fully lighted by the combined glares washing the compound, the uniped was using all three limbs to propel himself up the wall at a frantic rate. He seized the wall's upper edge, hoisted himself over, and vanished from sight in the mist that blew from the Rankor's moors of rock.

No one so much as fired a burst.

Dragonard held his breath. The implications stunned him.

They didn't shoot down the Solarian because they don't want the Solarian.

They shot Spellhands not because he was escaping, but because he was aiming to kill ME.

"There he is," a voice snapped on his right. A Regulator came diving out of the dark, slamming hard into him. Dragonard battered with both fists. He pulped a nose and felt blood spurt. They swarmed all over him and beat him, tough, expert, with none of their strength sapped by the hypnotic lights.

Dragonard went out, woke, went out again as

hands slung him upward along the alloy ladder into the Regulator skysled.

Lights went out. Were they in his head or in the compound? Hanging in a dark delirium, he felt lift. The skysled bearing him whipped toward the boiling Rankor night sky.

"All boats away clean," someone said. "What do we tell the Prison authorities?"

"We tell them nothing."

Dragonard recognized the second voice, opened his eyes, and saw a face swimming above, its tobacco-yellowed dragoon moustache drooped, curled, familiar. Old blue eyes watched, concerned.

The face belonged to his old superior, Sectioner of the Regulators Valk.

The jets whined. Dragonard felt them in his aching bones. The darkness kept pushing in from all sides. Valk's face crumbled like a shaken jigsaw puzzle. Dragonard knew he was being kidnapped, lofted from Rankor.

Why?

No answer.

Terrifying, bewildering, the dark foamed up a last time and drowned him.

IV

THE REGULATOR destroyer *Nuevo Athena* blurred in from hyperspace seven light years from the nearest II Galaxy planet. All engines stopped. The alarm fields raised and she lay hidden under the arch of giant red and purple and aquamarine suns.

In the fore saloon, with hatchways double-locked and armed guards outside, Dragonard ate his first decent meal in over two years.

He ate suspicion along with it. Sectioner Jonas Valk, old now, heavy in the middle, sat on a crescent-shaped lounge across from him. The flesh of Valk's leather-dark cheeks had lost its tone. Both of Valk's hands shook faintly.

"How much bitterness is left in you, Max?"

"A good deal."

Dragonard's face showed fatigue circles under the eyes. Otherwise he showed no reaction. He felt this was necessary until he learned the situation.

He'd wakened on the destroyer, his arms bearing the needle-marks of massive intravenous nutritional feedings. He did feel better. He was dressed in black Regulator fatigues which he'd had on when he woke up. Now he finished a bubble of brandy. Liquor burned his throat and belly, strange stuff after so long. But it was good.

He waited out the pause, then added, "Not bitterness with you, Jonas."

"God knows I tried in your behalf, even after you were sentenced."

"Yes, I heard."

"Three different appeals went no higher than the High Commander."

"No higher?"

"No higher."

"St. Anne felt the matter was closed?"

Valk nodded gravely. "There was the Regulator reputation to worry about. A good policeman creates a name for himself. It's inevitable with electronic communications, 'casts of news from all the palace cities. I know it was never really your fault, Max—the blackouts, the times when you went berserk. But manhandling suspects—"

Without tone, Dragonard interjected the words, "Who usually deserved it."

"It created special problems for us, all the same."

Abruptly Dragonard stood, tall, fierce-looking even though he stooped a little. His head nearly touched the clear canopy of the saloon. From where Valk sat, uncomfortable under Dragonard's accusing stare, the gold-eyed man looked like an awful giant. His hands hanging at his sides suggested killing power.

"I think I made it abundantly clear, Jonas, that I didn't want to carry the cross I carry."

"Of course, of course. The Regulators understood it was a birth defect. But—"

"How many times did I ask for proper medical attention?"

"Don't open the wounds that way, Max. There are other matters now, terrible—"

Valk's last word died, half-swallowed. Dragonard hardly heard.

"*You* brought up the subject of bitterness, Sectioner. I wanted the Lords of the Exchange to help me. I'd served the best I knew how, ever since I went to the Academy when I was twelve. Permission denied. That's exactly how they read me off. Techniques for surgical brain adjustment unavailable. Good God, I was a walking bomb! You could have transferred me—"

"You were too good a policeman, Max. The fine ones, smart and tough, are rare."

The acid of two years ate through all concern about why he was here. "And I caught the ring, didn't I? Tracked them. Unfortunately along with all the aphrodisiac ampules stockpiled in that casino, I caught the men who ran the ring, who distilled the ampules and sold them. Too bad for Max Dragonard that he happened to be a courtier's son, eh? He didn't need the credits. He was half rotted away with the drugs at eighteen. A fine specimen of manhood, yes?"

"Ah, Max." Valk sighed, gazing up through the canopy at the spangle of suns on the dark cloth of space. "A fine specimen. But with influence."

Dragonard couldn't even remember blacking out

during that particular attack. He remembered coming to in the casino as the red mist left his mind. What had been a squealing, amoral youngster who'd murdered maybe thousands with his drugs lay boneless and dead in front of him. All the young criminal's fine satins and his white fur tunic too showed red blood. It ran from Dragonard's fingers, a soft drip-drop onto the tips of his boots.

"If I'd killed some gutter idiot, it would have been different, Jonas."

"No doubt. But you're an adult. You know how the world works."

"It sends a man who wanted and asked for help to prison, for a crime he couldn't help committing."

"Yes, unfortunately. There was too much influence involved for St. Anne or any of us to help then."

Hands fisted, Dragonard took a lunging step back toward Valk. "Then how is it I've become socially acceptable all of a sudden? Has Thomas St. Anne turned bleeding-heart?"

Jonas Valk said in a low voice, "You know better. The High Commander of the Regulators is not aware of—what happened on Rankor. the men on this destroyer, the men with me on the sleds back there are all pledged to secrecy. They're loyal to me, Max, as you once were. What was done was done solely on my authority. No one else knows. God help us, it's dangerous but necessary." Valk's voice dropped even lower. Tiredness and something else sat hard on his shoulders. "I need you, Max. A strange thing is happening. A terrible thing—"

In Dragonard's mind a memory clicked. "Twice now you've said terrible."

"It is terrible."

Dragonard realized then that what sat so hard on Sectioner Jonas Valk was fear.

Cooling a little, feeling curious, Dragonard sat down. "Tell me."

Slowly Valk nodded. "I've thought long and painfully, Max, deciding what to do. A week ago I knew you were the one I needed. I had our staff espers peep you—I don't like to enter a man's mind that way but it had to be done. We learned about the escape the fellow with the mechanical hands had proposed to you. I ordered a continuous esper watch. We decided the cleanest, safest time to pull you free would be during the break itself. Once you decided to go along with the slaver, I moved the sleds into position. If that man's alive and tries to tell the prison authorities that Regulators picked you up, he won't be believed. We have you clear, I think."

"A kidnapping."

"Yes. If the break hadn't been planned, we would have broken you out ourselves." Valk looked up at the burning heavens. "Something terrible is happening, Max. No one in the Regulators knows what to do about it. Indeed, the damnable part is, we've gotten no orders at all from the Lords of the Exchange. There's a possibility that I could be cashiered or shot if what I've done is found out. But I really think St. Anne and the Lords would thank me, pension me nicely. The highest powers in II Galaxy are terrified, Max. Frozen, immobile. To protect the

Lords for whom I've worked all my life, I decided that I had to act on my own authority, in secret."

"I can't imagine what kind of thing you're talking about."

Valk's eyes looked spectral, moist with age at the corners.

"No, it's beyond your imagining. It was beyond mine, I know."

"Political upheaval?"

Jonas Valk reached for the serving bubble of brandy. He drank far too much in three gulps for a man his age. "Let me make my proposition first, Max."

"All right."

"Work for me on a mission. A secret one, unauthorized. At the conclusion, I'll spread the matter in the open, go right to St. Anne and tell him the whole thing and you'll have amnesty."

The word stunned Dragonard. He took the deepest breath in months.

"Everything wiped out?"

"Clean, Max. No more prison."

"Re-instated?"

"I'll try. That I can't promise. But no more cells."

"I do whatever it is, and if I succeed, *then* you go to St. Anne?"

"It can't be otherwise. If I went first I might be ordered to stop. Damn it"—what Valk said had a pitiful sound—"we don't know what's happening."

"I gamble for my freedom."

"Yes. It could be nasty. Dangerous."

A smile, at last, worked up the corners of Dragonard's mouth. "I still might kill someone."

"The esper watch went deep in you, Max. You've had no attacks since you were imprisoned."

"A few near misses. I hope maybe it's all over. God, I hope so."

"What's your answer?"

"I think it's fair that I know what I have to tackle."

A long hesitation. Jonas Valk twisted his fingers together.

"The kings are dying."

Dragonard's eyes went down to thin gold lines. "What are you saying?"

"I know, I know. I actually felt faint when the word came down the first time. But it's true. Xero of Hammansworld died a month ago, at age four hundred and three. Two weeks ago, Fomoko X succumbed in his sleep on Elder IV. He was barely ninety-nine. It simply doesn't happen, Max, as you and I both know. The Lords of the Exchange live an age at least. Eight or nine hundred years. It's part of the bloodlines, evidently."

Dragonard nodded. The average lifespan of a citizen of II Galaxy ranged from ninety-five to a hundred and thirty. To be told that a star king perished before his eight hundredth year literally tore a man's whole cosmos of belief apart. Dragonard had lived under a hierarchy of near-deathless monarchs since his childhood.

"The Lords have the finest medicine available," Dragonard said, trying to bring reason out of the disorder of the revelation. "No ordinary man could begin to afford the staff of physicians attending them." He said it without rancor. Many times he'd questioned the smaller system within which he'd operated, the tough, well-disciplined world of the Regulators. But the Lords of the Exchange were a rank apart. Their right to wealth and privilege was unquestioned. Their succumbing to the afflictions which killed ordinary men was unthinkable.

"Evidently the doctors can do nothing. It's all very hush-hush. Just fragments reach me in reports. Xero and Fomoko II are dead, others are gravely ill on a dozen of the worlds. The counselors of the Lords are doing nothing either. No one knows what malady is striking, or why. Paralysis has us all tight, like this." Valk made a fist. "If it's a plot, no one will admit it's a plot. St. Anne refuses to discuss it with me or anyone. No one's sleeping. There's terror, terror and uncertainty as never before."

Dragonard helped himself to more brandy. This time, he felt he needed it.

"And you've taken it upon yourself, Jonas, to try to find an answer?"

"Yes. This God-damnable inaction will destroy II Galaxy if it goes on. Word will spread—"

"You have no orders? You're a brave man."

Jonas Valk shook his head. "Not at my age. A loyal one. The Lords of the Exchange are my lords. Yours, too. They would have helped you if they could have."

Melancholy now, Dragonard stared into his

brandy. He found it easy to say, "Yes, I suppose so."

"Don't help me out of loyalty to them if you don't feel it, Max. I put it to you in terms of self-interest."

"To make sure I take you up?"

"Of course."

"What am I supposed to do, for God's sake, if all the Regulators are balked?"

"It's tenuous. A suspicion only. A rumor. You'll go to Pentagon."

Into Dragonard's mind leaped a sharp image of the huge, savage world he'd visited once on a case. Pentagon was a forlorn and primitive planet with but a few barbaric cities. The armor and munitions factories of the Lords of the Exchange were located there, simply because the volatile materials which they handled were too dangerous to be processed on more populous worlds. Dragonard had a memory of gibbous white moons, crags, sandy wastes, dry dead lakes and crumbled castles that had housed proud fighting princes in the long-ago before the devastating wars.

"In past months," Valk went on, "we've had a bit of puzzling intelligence from Pentagon. Talk of a secret terroristic society. Some call it a small army. The ships going into Pentagon carry scum these days. Mercenary soldiers, pardoned criminals, the dregs. They disappear into the North Wastes. To what purpose no one knows, unless it's to join this movement or army."

Now Dragonard scoffed with a laugh. "A few

criminal revolutionaries organizing on a planet that's hardly out of the iron age? What damage could they do?"

Valk gestured with trembling fingers. "That's the riddle, Max."

"That's what you want me to try to find out?"

"Yes. As an outcast, a man who wants to join them."

"Who's running this phantom army?"

"An anonymous leader. Never seen. But they have a flag. It's been seen a few times when bands of these scum have foraged in the villages. The flag's scarlet, usually nothing more than a red rag. Sewn on it is a heart, a human shaped heart, but made of diamond or crystal or some other material obviously synthetic and transparent. In the center of the heart there's a tangle of yellow wire that glows like gold. We have sketches in the vidfiles if you want to see. Police artist jobs but reasonably accurate, I am informed. This flag gives them their name. The Heart Flag movement."

"Heart Flag." It had a murmurous, defiant sound. "What's it mean?"

"We don't know. Neither do we know whether there is any real connection with what is happening to the Lords. But one thing makes it worth following up. It made me want your services badly enough to break you out. See it this way, now: the star kings, men who never age, men who never grow ill but simply disappear at the appointed time of succession—they're dying. We don't know whether they ever died before. Presumably they did, but in secret, at a very old age. Now they are dying young and semi-publicly and there's this Heart Flag movement with an unknown leader who chooses to style himself with a name that might be significant."

"What is it?"

"Methuselah."

Dragonard looked at the stars above the canopy and chuckled, wolfish, pleased.

"All right, Jonas. I'll go. I'd sooner die free on Pentagon than mold on Rankor."

"So I thought, Max."

Sectioner Valk reached for a call tube and ordered engines full ahead into hyperdrive.

V

A WEEK LATER, Dragonard boarded *Illyria Anne* at the capital spaceport on Rimmini.

That is, a man bearing papers which identified him as Minor Hastings, a jeweller by craft, got aboard and stowed his meager gear in the tiny, sour F-class cabin. The papers of Minor Hastings gave a physical description which conformed to Dragonard's. Under *Distinguishing marks, other* the magnetic numerals were encoded for the pierced left ear and short white chin scar which Valk's cosmeticians had operated onto him.

Dragonard wore a small, brilliant synthetic sapphire in his earlobe. Ordinary people considered such ornamentation foppish, but in the Xanthors sun system, of which Rimmini was the largest planet, an ear sapphire was the underworld's recognition sign for a freelance jewel thief available for hire.

Dragonard had worked with Jonas Valk for three days at an abandoned villa on the outskirts of the capital. A few techs Valk could trust, the cosmeticians and document specialists, prepared his cover. A night news bulletin interrupted one session. The announcer reported that the Lord of the Xanthors, Cunardo IX, was canceling all further ceremonial appearances.

Unsurprised, Valk nodded. "My runners brought the information before noon."

"He's dying too?"

"Yes. The palace is shut off to any but the Lord's intimates. It's spreading, Max. We've booked your passage to Pentagon for Tuesday dusk. It can be none too soon."

Dragonard stayed in his cabin until *Illyria Anne* blasted free and went into hyperdrive for the seventy-two-hour relative time journey. Around midnight a wall speaker announced that the Grand Concourse and Casino were open for gaming and buffet suppers. He hauled his black cloak with the peacock-pattern lining from a peg and slung it on. Then he adjusted the hip-strap of the dress rapier. He whicked the blade twice in the air. Excellent metal, although the scabbard enameling and the basket-hilt goldplate were cheap.

In a floating mirror Dragonard gave himself a sardonic wink as he went out. The Regulators knew how to turn a man into what he was supposed to be; in this case a professional thief with a taste for gaudy clothes, but a formidable looking man for all that. The scar made him sinister, and his gold eyes heightened the effect. Dragonard's boots thrummed as he strode to the lift stairs. *Illyria Anne* was too old, and too shabby a star-run, to be equipped with gravtubes.

Perhaps two hundred people gambled on the floor

of the Grand Concourse and Casino. Dragonard drifted among them, sorted them into two principal types: first, dreary, conventionally dressed munitions engineers whose work took them to the Pentagon arsenals regularly; second, a smaller contingent of nervous-eyed men and women from an assortment of planets, probably antique thieves, confidence artists on the dodge—Pentagon wrote no extradition treaties—and stolen property handlers going to peddle their wares in the white markets of the old cities beside the empty seabeds.

He walked among them with a put-on swagger, ignoring the invitations of the croupiers. In one dim corner, under a canopy of moulding dark red velvet, a serious high-stakes game of jitterdice was in progress.

The men involved were drably dressed, pale and narrow-cheeked. They watched the nine cubes dancing on the baize bottom of the box with great intensity. The free molecules in the last three dice came to rest. The dice dropped. Saying nothing, one thin man smoking a cigar pushed plaques to the winner on his right.

Before moving on Dragonard counted at least fifty thousand in plaques.

The players were professional criminals who carried side arms, made no noise, and drew no attention to themselves. This was in contrast to the drunken blabber of the antiques men who preferred the cheap payoffs of the rickety solid-slots.

The thin man with the cigar glanced up as Dragonard passed. The man squinted through smoke, looked at the table. Dragonard raised one hand palm out, dropped it. The man glanced away.

But Dragonard felt reassured; he'd been invited into the high-stakes group. That indicated he was recognizable as a type. His cover identified him, and well. His gesture had signaled that he might join later, and the man's looking away meant Dragonard was free to come in when he wished.

For the first time since the big thrusters boomed, carrying the ship off, Dragonard enjoyed a breath of relief. He was as safe, as camouflaged as he could be.

He had no way to defend himself against identification by an esper, of course. Jonas Valk had no psych-blockers he could fully trust. On the other hand, Valk said he had no reason to assume that Dragonard would be tracked by police espers, either. The Regulators wouldn't be looking for an agent on a mission initiated, against all rules, by one of their own.

A curving staircase led up to the Grand Concourse lounge. Dragonard took a table in the badly lit bar. From this point on the balcony he could survey the pit.

Weak light-globes floated in a narrow orbit around the area of tiny tables. Except for a man and woman fondling in the darkest rear corner, Dragonard was alone. A Barthoman with a large, globular head took his order.

He nursed two drinks along for half an hour. Then, just as he was preparing to pay, the beautiful blonde girl walked up the staircase.

Dragonard recalled seeing her in the pit earlier. At least he remembered the costume she wore. Of vertical strings of diffraction beads, it shimmered with all the colors of the spectrum. In contrast to last year's fashion, the girl's bosom was covered. Otherwise the gown revealed much more than it concealed. She had a splendid body, high-breasted and lithe. Her yellow hair shone. She was achingly young, no more than twenty-five at most.

She put her bag on the bar and picked a solitary stool. Over her shoulder she glanced at Dragonard.

Neither coy nor provocative, her stare sought information. Dragonard grinned. Her return smile was honest, unoffended.

"My pleasure, please," he called to the dozing Barthoman.

As the bartender poured her wine, Dragonard stood. He indicated the empty seat at his table.

The girl took her glass and bag and walked toward him. Her face was lovely, composed. She seemed neither shocked nor excited at having a man buy her a drink.

"Thanks," she said as she sat down. "This is a cheap, dull ship. I only dressed and came in here on the hope that there might be some conversation available."

Dragonard's gold eyes danced as a light-globe floated past his head. "Conversation?"

"That's all I had in mind, yes." Her blue eyes were no-nonsense.

"You talk as though you've ridden this tin tub before."

"About once a month. I'm a clerk courier in the munitions inventory office."

Dragonard tapped the wide silver bracelet on her left wrist. "And those three interlinked rings are the sign of someone native-born to Pentagon."

She sipped wine. "Yes, my father came out as a career officer. I've never left. I don't know why. Lack of initiative, probably."

"A girl as attractive as you should find plenty of men willing to supply initiative."

"On Pentagon? Have you ever been there?"

Dragonard tried to look suitably evasive. "This is my first trip."

"A few small enclaves of civilized life. That means with apartments that have pure water in the pipes, and electrical lights. The rest of it's barbaric. I hate the stink of those wild men who stamp around the streets on those awful monsters they ride. Greasy hair to their shoulders, swords as long as that, leather harness—it's disgusting." Then she caught herself, smiled, and the loveliness of her blue eyes stung him again. "I'm Kristin, by the way."

"Ah—Minor Hastings."

"What takes you to Pentagon?"

"A short vacation."

"You don't mind if I don't believe you?"

Dragonard's lips peeled back. "I don't mind. That is, unless you're a police spy."

Kristin moistened her lips. They were painted a frosty white, the vogue among the few women in II Galaxy who could afford personal cosmetics. "You're certainly frank."

"No point in being otherwise now. When we went into hyper, we passed the extradition line."

"Was it that bad for you on Rimmini?"

"Let's just say that a short absence looked prudent. For the record, I'm on my way to Gannonblock, the munitions port, to make a jewelry appraisal."

Now Kristin's laugh tinkled merrily. "Oh, you're delightful. There are no jewels at Gannonblock, or on the whole dirty, barbaric planet for that matter. Unless you count the rocks some of the North Waste barbarians wear on those gut strings around their necks."

"No jewels?" Dragonard was mocking. "I've been misinformed."

"I won't tell anyone. Enjoy your vacation." She reached for her bag.

"Let me buy you another drink."

"Well, one more."

They chatted about the run-down condition of *Illyria Anne* until the next round came. Then she asked several personal questions: his birthplace; what he thought of Cunardo IX canceling his appearance; how long he had been on Rimmini. Dragonard was evasive. He'd already sketched his background sufficiently. Unless she were a fool, which he suspected she wasn't, she should know now that he was a man on the run, involved with jewelry illegally, and wanting it left at that. So he fended the questions, laughed or spoke some vague sarcasm.

She crossed her legs. Her breasts gleamed under

the spectrum-shining beads. God almighty, she was lovely.

"Pentagon seems to be a haven for criminals these days," she said.

"Tell me again, Kristin. Do you really have no police relatives?"

She gave him a level stare. "I'm sorry. I was only thinking out loud. There has been talk in the munitions compounds, that's all. And on my last few trips I've noticed a different class of men riding in. Before, the passengers were mostly engineers or couriers."

Carefully, Dragonard said, "You live there. If there's an influx, what's the reason?"

"I don't know." She concentrated on her wine a little too studiously. "I didn't mean to offend you."

"You didn't."

He touched her hand. She didn't draw away but her flesh was cool. His own fingers hurt. Two years on Rankor caused it. No pretty girl to touch, to smell as he smelled her now, soap-fresh yet lightly perfumed. He hadn't seen a woman in far too long a time.

Yet he wasn't entirely satisfied with that explanation. His overwhelming reaction to her beauty surprised and troubled him. How did he know what she was?

"It's no secret men have hidden in the Pentagon Wastes before," Kristin was saying. "Yet nowadays you see so many of that kind of man. On the street corners—at the inn yards hiring beasts and then riding off on the roads up-country. New ones turn up every day. The number of them stays about the same in the city as the others leave. Almost as though''—here she paused, drinking her wine to the dregs—''someone were hiring them for a purpose.''

Dragonard's nerves tightened up. Little silent alarms brought him to full alert.

So she rode the ship regularly, did she? He could be closer than he'd suspected. A single word repeated itself in his mind.

Recruiter.

''Well,'' he laughed, patting her hand again, ''I can assure you nobody's offered me any credits to do a damn thing on Pentagon. Come on, one more and then I'm turning in.''

She glanced down at his fingers lying on top of hers. She glanced up, her blue eyes large and compelling. He noticed for the first time that her cheeks had turned pink. Quickly she drew her hand away, as though she'd felt what he felt, and been concerned about it.

''You're a very persuasive man, Hastings. Yes, I'll have another.''

They drank. Dragonard pulled a thin gold-filled stylus from his black weskit. He shoved it across, along with one of the discarded drinking napkins.

''I'd appreciate it if you'd write the name of a decent inn.''

''They're all brawling, noisy places, I'm afraid. Keep your sword handy.''

He accepted that, drew the napkin back, and began to draw idle scribbles. He drew a whorl. A triangle. A square. A credit sign. Then, watching her closely, he drew a rectangle whose lines were not quite straight.

In the center of the flag shape he sketched a heart.

Drinking, she watched. Her breathing didn't accelerate; her eyes didn't widen. If she recognized the Heart Flag, she gave no sign.

Perhaps he'd scared her off.

She rose, one thigh shining briefly among the beads. "I must go. I've enjoyed it though."

"We'll still be aboard tomorrow night. I'd like to see you again, Kristin."

"Yes, all right." She looked at him and he felt warm. "I'd like that too, Hastings."

Turning, she left in a glitter of scintillant beads. Dragonard stared at the flag he'd drawn. If she knew what it meant, she hadn't let on in the least. Would she tomorrow night, perhaps?

She was so damn beautiful, he hated himself for suspecting her.

VI

THE NEXT NIGHT Dragonard waited three hours for Kristin. She never appeared.

In a booth off the Grand Concourse bar he dialed the ship's central passenger exchange. He requested a connection with the girl's cabin.

"We are very sorry, sir," replied the machine's metallic voice.

"What do you mean?"

"We have a signal posted, sir. She does not wish to be disturbed."

Puzzled and angry, Dragonard punched the wipe-out key. He walked back to the bar and ordered another liquor, his head already feeling faintly fuzzy from the last ones. He tossed the drink down in three gulps. Then he strolled down into the Casino.

Had he scared Kristin off by drawing the Heart Flag? Had she suspected him of being a police agent? If so, the result was ironic and infuriating.

As Dragonard moved toward the dark corner where the pale men sat at their jitterdice game, he reminded himself that personal involvement with any woman now would be dangerous. His freedom or his life would be forfeit if he fouled up. Damn it, why couldn't she have been an ordinary traveler?

He was certain another identity hid behind her public one. Just his luck.

Valk had supplied him with a generous credit account. Maybe dice for high stakes would wipe the image of her blue eyes from the back of his brain.

Dragonard stopped at the table where the five players sat.

"Chair open?"

The thin man smoking a cigar dumped the nine dice back into the agitator. "Thousand minimum."

"I think I can make it." Dragonard threw a small sheaf of credits down.

Two of the other players appraised him. One looked at the star sapphire in his earlobe, smiling. None of them missed it. The cigar smoker, tough and slightly built, spun the dial of the agitator box.

A faint hum indicated that the field inside the box was disarranging the dice molecules. One of the others pulled a plush chair from the corner. Dragonard settled into it.

"My name is Karl," said the cigar smoker. He didn't shake hands.

"Minor Hastings," Dragonard said with a nod of his head.

The rest introduced themselves either with first names only, or with obvious aliases. The player to Dragonard's right had a wart on his nose, and said his name was Robert Smith. Dragonard chuckled. It broke the momentary tension. Karl snickered out loud and knocked the ash from his cigar. He ground the ash on the stained maroon carpet under his boot heel.

Then Karl banked, exchanging Dragonard's first thousand for plaques. Karl wore a stainless steel chronometer on a link chain around his neck. Examining the watch, he ticked his nail against the dial. Then he looked directly at Dragonard.

"So nobody misunderstands, Hastings, we quit at three. No sooner. No later."

Dragonard didn't much like the man's flat, unfriendly assertiveness. "Suppose I'm on a streak and feel like getting up before that."

"Then pick up your credits and don't play," growled the wart-nosed Terran on his right.

"That's the size of it," Karl agreed. "You asked for the chair."

Dragonard scowled. Finally he nodded. Karl gestured to the agitator box.

"Since you just came in, the dice are yours. Bets down, gentlemen."

Pushing two plaques out in front of him, Dragonard said, "Two hundred on thirty-or-less."

One player bet with Dragonard; two bet against him. Karl bet two hundred on forty-or-more. Dragonard reached over to snap the lever of the agitator box. Its front trap flew open and the nine dice spun down the chute into the baize-lined box which measured a foot square.

The dice banged and rattled and ricocheted against the cushioned sides. The free molecules in the first die came to rest. The die flopped down with a three-spot showing.

Karl appeared uninterested as the second and third dice stopped. He leaned back in his chair, puffing smoke and watching the ceiling. He wound the watch on the neck-chain idly.

Like white bullets the dice banged and clattered on the box walls. Finally the ninth die fell. The man with the warty nose grinned.

"Six, six, five, three, four, five, four, three and a six."

Karl shifted the cigar in his mouth. "I make that forty-two." With a little smirk at Dragonard, he raked in the plaques. "Your dice, Golly," he said to wart-nose.

The players didn't indulge in polite conversation. A tense silence pervaded the table. On the next play Dragonard bet forty-or-more himself. So did Karl. They won and the pot was split in half. The third play Dragonard took by himself with a risky under-twenty.

From the next play onward, Dragonard lost steadily. More often than not Karl took the winnings. The wart-nosed man, Golly, amassed the second largest pot and the other players won occasionally. Karl enjoyed himself, leaning back and winding his watch every other play or so.

At the end of forty minutes a steamy anger had built up inside Dragonard. He watched the last of the nine dice come to rest. Karl read off their spots aloud, then said, "Forty-four again. Not your night, Hastings. Bad luck."

Karl's thin-boned hands swept across the table to pull in the plaques. All at once Dragonard's right hand came up from the table, caught the other man's wrist and held it tight.

"Let's leave them there just a second." Dragonard's eyes looked tiger-yellow in the low light.

Karl clamped his teeth tight on his cigar. "Let go of me, mister."

To his right Dragonard sensed rather than saw Golly shift his chair. The wart-nosed man's shoulder drooped slightly. Dragonard knew he'd moved his hand close to his side arm.

With a smile Dragonard uncurled his fingers. Karl sat rigid as he chafed his wrist. He glared.

"Those are my winnings, mister. You're not trying to dispute that, are you?"

Dragonard said nothing. A career in police work had its advantages. You knew the dodges and the devices that criminals used. Probably Karl hadn't been employing his little helper during the game with his friends. At least Dragonard hadn't seen him using it earlier. Karl had taken him for a jewel thief who'd know nothing about gambling manipulation tricks, and so had started using the helper after he sat down.

Dragonard remained silent a moment. Then he scooped up all the dice. He dumped them in the agitator box.

"What the hell do you think you're doing?" Karl demanded.

The box hummed. "Just seeing how improbable the laws of probability can get in a friendly game like this."

Golly's right hand dropped. Dragonard's right hand flashed, digging into the man's lower left arm, biting deep. Golly grunted, sweat breaking out on his cheeks and chin.

"Lift your other hand up on the table or I'll break this one for you," Dragonard said.

Spitting an obscenity under his breath, Golly writhed in his chair. Dragonard dug deeper with his fingers.

Golly's right hand rose to view, away from his side arm. He slapped it hard on the table.

Dragonard let go. He reached over toward the agitator box which had stopped humming and sprung the dice loose down the shute. They bulleted and ricocheted at blinding speed off the walls of the box. Just as the last three were falling to a stop, Dragonard lunged up out of his chair and across the table. With one quick wrench he snapped the silver chain around Karl's neck.

The table froze. Dragonard loomed tall, twisting the winder of the chronometer once, twice, three times.

In the baize-lined box the nine dice leaped, banged and clicked against the box walls.

Dragonard stopped winding. The dice clattered down to rest.

Dragonard held the chronometer between thumb and forefinger. It sparkled like a silver wafer.

"A miniaturized auxillary control field. You should have tried it on someone else, Karl. Someone who hasn't seen one before."

He dropped the watch to the rug, lifted his boot and smashed down with the heel.

The watch case crumbled, disintegrated. Dragonard reached for his plaques. His anger was passing. He'd made his point.

Karl hovered half in, half out of his chair. His eyes were sooty, angry circles. Dragonard touched the plaques. Karl's hand dropped fast toward his waist.

Dragonard kicked the chair over behind him. He jumped to one side and pulled on the basket-hilt of the rapier. Out came the blade, thin, shining, a whisper of metal cutting the air.

"That chron cost me a multicredit, you—"

Karl called Dragonard filthy names. His hand crossed his waist suddenly, bypassing the blaster on his right hip and pulling at the hilt of his enameled throw-knife in its scabbard. Dragonard lunged out, driving the rapier toward Karl's right shoulder.

Golly caught his arm and hauled it down. Cursing, Dragonard smashed the man's wart-nose with his elbow. Karl backed against the wall. He whipped his arm back, then forward.

The throw-knife blurred. Dragonard twisted his head so hard his neck hurt, but the maneuver saved him from losing an eye. The blade ripped across his cheek, tearing flesh away, bringing blood. It gushed down warm onto his shoulder.

Suddenly Dragonard found himself hampered: Golly grabbed his right arm and tried to crack it over his knee; the player on his left kicked at his shins; Karl circled the table, snatched up his knife. A sudden babble of loud voices from the Casino floor said that other passengers were aware of the fight now. Dragonard swept out with the rapier again as Karl crouched, knife winking in his right hand.

Karl panted. His unkempt hair hung in his eyes. He parried as Dragonard drove in. Karl caught the taller man's basket hilt on the thicker hilt of the throw-knife. Karl was strong. He heaved. Dragonard was off balance and he staggered backward. Golly smashed a chair against the small of his back.

Pain burst in Dragonard's spine like a hot flower.

He righted himself and spun around, dropping into a crouch. At the edges of his mind a thin reddish haze swept in like a sea. It grew brighter until it obscured everything but Karl's face. Dragonard's shoulders shook and his gold eyes shone. His lips peeled back from his teeth like an animal's.

The redness dominated him, blurring everything but Karl's face. Karl hesitated, watching the awful change come over the tall man. Like melting wax Dragonard's veneer of civility dropped away. Underneath remained a face of death, gold eyes that shone without sense.

Yelling, Dragonard leaped forward. He slashed Karl's cheek open with the rapier. Karl screamed and tried to get out of the way. His screams dinned in Dragonard's ears. A lovely sound.

Karl's face loomed larger, whiter, washed by the redness Dragonard knew was in his own mind. For one instant he was aware of what he was doing, and tried to stop himself. But the pain in his cut cheek and battered backbone had triggered him like a bomb.

He was aware of Karl screaming and screaming;

aware of passengers shouting in confusion; aware of Golly trying to stay his arm as he dove in bodily against Karl, ramming the rapier ahead. Karl stumbled. Otherwise the rapier would have pierced his throat. It buried in the wall and snapped.

Dragonard caught Karl around the throat as the red fire lit up all of his mind.

A drunken, sweet feeling filled him as he choked Karl, choked, choked, *choked*. . . .

Voices babbled.

Hands tore at him.

Dragonard heard, felt, saw nothing—

Nothing except the face of Karl, the face he hated and had to ruin. . . .

Emerging from the nauseous darkness, Dragonard shuddered with a violent, fever-like chill.

An assistant purser hovered by his bunk. Dragonard sat up. His throat was parched. The purser backed off a couple of paces. Dragonard's teeth chattered. His sour little cabin smelled of his own sweat. He recognized in the trembling and the stink the aftermath of a seizure.

Dark circles blotted his eyesockets as he clutched the bunk stanchion. He was almost afraid to ask what had happened. The purser stared at him as though he were some kind of animal.

Finally: "The man I attacked. Is he—?"

"We pulled you off of him, Mr. Hastings; you'd have killed him. You were choking him. It took four of us to drag you down here." Nervously the man indicated a report pad in his hand. "I have to file a report. There'll be charges for damages to the furnishings—"

"Is he alive?" Dragonard was hoarse. "Damn it, tell me!"

"Yes. Yes, sir. His friends are taking care of him."

"He cheated me at dice. When I caught him, he attacked me. I must have had too much to drink. I lost my head." Fiercely Dragonard stared. "That's all there is to it. I'll pay for the damages." Something compelled him to repeat, "That's all there is to it."

In the purser's eyes shone an uncertainty which said that wasn't all there was to it by any manner of means. Dragonard covered his eyes with one hand and leaned against the bunk. Nausea and chill shook him. The purser extended his pad. He looked terrified. Like a man inside a cage with a beast, Dragonard thought.

And isn't he?

"Please, sir, I—need your signature. The bill will include the medical spray the doctor used to dress the wound in your cheek."

Reaching out with fingers that shook, Dragonard took the stylus. He signed.

"Get out of here," he said, hiding his face.

"Sir, the captain needs this report to indicate why—"

Whirling, Dragonard yelled, "I told you! I was drunk and he jumped me." His hands balled at his sides without his willing it. A sickly pallor whitened his face. In the cabin's poor light his eyes shone like heated coins. "I'll pay for everything. That's all the report you need. Now get the hell out of here."

The assistant purser thrust the pad under his arm and raced for the door with a feeble salute.

The door shut, clanging. Dragonard leaned against the bunk stanchion. His shoulders heaved with chill.

It had happened again.

It had happened again.

And he'd hoped against hope he was done with it.

Why was his mind faulty? Why couldn't it be repaired? Damn it, *why?*

Illyria Anne hummed faintly in hyperdrive. Dragonard flicked off the one lonely light and huddled in the dark, knowing the worst. He was sick, as sick as he'd ever been. The seizures hadn't stopped at all. They would never stop until the day he tried to kill someone and was shot down. He couldn't help what he did. Violence, anger triggered it. But that changed nothing.

All through the prison time he'd lived with false hope. He would never be cured. And now, when he finally had a chance to straighten things out, fight for an amnesty, this had to happen. He had to find out *now* of all times that it was hopeless.

Shuddering, he hung on the bunk stanchion. If he hadn't been a man he would have wept.

VII

WHEN THE LINER docked at Gannonblock, Dragonard joined the crowds on the down gangways. He expected to see Karl and Golly and their companions. His fingers weren't far from the basket-hilt of the rapier he'd purchased in *Illyria Anne's* passenger shop. The metal was poorer than that of the sword Valk had provided, but it would still gore someone after revenge.

As the passengers waited turns at customs in the high-roofed, chilly sheds, Dragonard watched carefully. He saw nothing of Karl and the others. But there were eleven customs lines open. Missing them would be easy unless they wanted to seek him out.

Apparently they didn't.

An official checked Dragonard's papers and valise. That was when Dragonard spotted a cerulean blue cloak four queues down, its thrown-back cowl mostly hidden by hair like gilt foam.

"Kristin!" Dragonard shouted. "Kristin, this way!"

The girl stiffened. She heard him but didn't turn around. Dragonard grabbed his valise.

"'Not finished,'' the official said, hauling the bag back to stamp it.

He took his time about doing it. With an unfriendly glance, he finally released the bag. He hadn't missed the star sapphire in Dragonard's earlobe.

Dragonard snatched up the valise and plunged running into the noisy crowd.

After ten minutes of searching in the huge, chilly sheds he knew he'd lost her.

Pentagon was older than the recorded history of II Galaxy. Those native-born to it clung to their primitive ways. Dragonard saw a group of Pentagon men swinging along the offal-strewn cobbled street outside the relatively modern spaceport. The men stood tall, with thick shoulders, flat-nosed faces. Clearly of Terran descent, they had let their environment brutalize them, or retard their progress, or both. They wore leather fighting harness. Their arms and grimy ankles jingled with fighter's rings, primitively beautiful bracelets of bronze that bore crude representations of battle, drinking or lovemaking. Two of them carried spears, the others broadswords.

One of the group tugged the tether rope of a riding-beast native to the planet. The animal stood three hands higher than the largest horse Dragonard could remember seeing in a museum. Its hide glistened, scaled and hard. Four clawed pads thudded on the cobbles as its drunken master led it along. The beasts gave off a leathery smell that Dragonard soon discovered permeated the thin, oxygenated, high mountain-type air.

The beasts provided universal transportation on Pentagon. No formal, modern transportation existed between Pentagon's few scattered cities on its three arid and inhospitable continents. The city of Gannonblock was the largest of the old towns, approaching a million and a half population. It sprawled over ten hills at the southern tip of Northmark, the largest continent. Southward, a dead sea-bottom bedeviled with dust storms stretched away.

From a hilltop where he'd walked, Dragonard observed a few flickering lights out over the empty sea. Further out, a red smudge swept half the horizon. The lights were the running lamps of small skysleds belonging to the munitions works, an official installation.

Dragonard stood in the dry wind, savoring the smells of leather and spices and dung. The first of the triple moons rose. By its white light he could make out the endless rows of pollution exchangers rising far out in the dead sea. They glowed like red-tipped styli, thrusting up like ancient smokestacks Dragonard had seen in picture books. Their redness marked the lower heavens.

Gannonblock proper seemed to consist of teetering, many-storied buildings that crawled everywhich-way over the hillsides. Dragonard walked back down the hill and darkness plunged around him, relieved only here and there by the blue flare of chemical torches stuck in niches. A woman asked whether he'd like to share her favors.

He turned, shaking his head, and responded in the Common Tongue which she'd used. Where she was half hidden in a dark doorway, metal gleamed, the metal of a knife in some bagsnatcher's hand.

Dragonard's gold eyes flashed in the torch reflection. There was a stunned cessation of noise and movement in the doorway as the light limned his features. Dragonard smiled and walked on.

He found an acceptable inn, ate an acceptable meal and slept an unacceptable sleep haunted by images of Kristin. Down in the inn yard, tethered beasts brayed and stamped. Primitive stringed instruments and hide drums twanged and thrummed from the common room until moonset and after. Several fights broke out. Once Dragonard rose, kicked open the shutters of his cubicle and started to lean out to yell for a little quiet.

What stopped him was the sight of three drably dressed Terrans emerging from the common room directly below. They talked hardly at all. Two wore beards and red boots.

It had been years since he'd seen professional assassins flaunt their occupation with the red-boot symbol. This gave him some idea of the tenuous hold law and order had on Gannonblock and Pentagon. The men left the inn yard.

Were they Heart Flag recruits?

Far over the jumbled rooftops, the last of the triple moons dropped whitely behind crags, etching them. Those were the North Wastes. Out there lay his answer. He closed the shutters, shivering.

Next day Dragonard roamed the seamier quarters.

He had no trouble striking up conversations with some of the men who made no secret of being fugitives. His clothes and the star sapphire and his general bearing identified him well enough as one of the pack.

Dragonard sat over a tankard in a sidewalk grogpit just before sundown. His companion was a fat, bald rogue who kept up a lively conversation about the nymphs of Pentagon for several minutes and then fell to dozing on his arms. His snores made the empty tankards rattle on the wood.

"Perhaps you can give me a little guidance, friend," Dragonard said.

The fat man lifted his head and let out a loose, blubbering sound. He had only one good eye; his left shone pink. Thick-grown tissue ridged with scars covered the socket.

"I come all the way from Korfu's World, mister, and I learned pretty quick that a couple of brews don't buy you much in Gannonblock."

"All I want is a steer in the right direction. I'm looking for some people. I hear they pay well for men who can use weapons."

The fat man lowered his head again after licking his lips. "Wouldn't know."

"I'm looking," Dragonard persisted, "for an old man with an old name."

"You're lucky to live two days on this rotten planet," said the fat man from behind his arms. He made some blubbering sounds. "Slit you for mini-credits, they will. Also for talking too much. Which I can't do anyway, bein' this terrible thirst is gripping me."

Dragonard waved to the grogkeeper. He passed over several credit notes.

"Bring my friend another and keep bringing them as long as that lasts."

When the keeper went away, the fat man lifted his head. His scarred eyesocket looked ghoulish in the purple shadow-light settling over the street. High in the earth-walled apartment building across the way, someone screamed. No one paid the slightest attention.

"Very generous," said the fat man. "Thankee. Or are you law?"

"If I were would I want to find Methuselah?"

The silence was pierced only by the thudding of three riders cantering along on beasts. The tankard arrived. With shuddering hands the fat man drained it in continuous gulps and called for another.

"Yes, you've the look of killer on you, if I know it." The fat man glanced both ways and belched. "The Sign of the Starfish. Easy to find. Ask anyone."

Dragonard lidded his gold eyes in acknowledgment and melted into the stinking dusk.

The Sign of the Starfish thundered with drums. Smoke coiled, almost graspable. From within it, small oily lights flashed, the flames of cheap ornamental lamps on the tiny tables.

You reached The Sign of the Starfish by going down six stairs, dodging through a long open tunnel beneath one of the towering apartments, and jumping across an open sewer that bubbled with running filth in a walled courtyard. A man of Pentagon wrapped in a cloak manned the door. Dragonard wasn't even stopped.

He sat at a cramped little table with a watery beer at his elbow. The other occupants packed into the crowded, low-ceilinged room were so many shadows. Between thuds of the drum, he caught snatches of conversation in a dozen tongues, with much cursing.

Irritably, Dragonard wondered how he'd find anyone to ask about the Heart Flag in this octopus-like dark where bodies, faces, arms were sensed rather than seen. A sudden white light blazed up, hurting his eyes—a chemical torch.

The waiter had shoved him up to this table at the very edge of a small, circular stone platform which was raised slightly above the level of the floor. The sputtering chemical torch had been thrust through a curtain to the rear of this stone circle. The arm which held it was brown, muscled. The torch threw off silver sparks, glaring as brilliantly as an electrical searchlight.

Dragonard saw his surroundings by its light—a darkwalled place packed with coarse men of all breeds and skin-colors, all of them drinking hard. Two individuals in full black robes with high cowls looked at him briefly from the packed bar. In the spark-sputter, their eyes shone out from the cowls and then vanished as the torch dimmed a little.

A reed pipe joined the thrumming of the invisible drummer. Through the tattered curtain a shapely white feminine leg thrust like a sword. Men sucked in their breath, a noise of wind.

Bells tinkled, minor, discordant. They clattered as

the girl swooped the curtain behind her and leaped to the middle of the stone stage.

The torchman moved out behind her. Flat-nosed, with greasy hair hanging to his shoulders, he stared into space and held the brand aloft.

The girl poised in the shifting silver light, her body trembling. Her costume consisted of a single wide leather strap looped around the nape of her neck. The ends of the strap hung down between her breasts, reaching her knees. On the strap hung dozens of bells, several large, most small or tiny. As the girl's legs began to move, picking up the drum-rap, the bells rang.

Her head bobbed around in a rhythmic circle. She wore a black kerchief which concealed her nose, her eyes and all of her hair.

A dryness tickled Dragonard's throat. The planes of the girl's body flashed silvery, then black as she began to dance. In each hand she held a pair of finger cymbals. The leather strap flew back and forth. The bells jangled faintly, then more loudly. Their ringing set up weird reverberations. Between the jingling of the bells, the girl touched her finger cymbals together, little grace notes in the clatter.

The sensuality of the dance reached Dragonard quickly. It reached everyone else too. Men craned forward. Dragonard heard the scrape of fingernails itching chin stubble. The drums thudded; the pipe skirled; the leather strap flew, bells clashing.

All at once the girl wrenched her body to a stop, back bowed. She trembled. Then her finger cymbals tinkled as she leaped back into the wild, amoral pattern of the dance.

She began to dance in a circle, round and round the perimeter of the stone platform. The bell-straps stood out from her body as she flew by. One of them flicked Dragonard's chin. The silver light shifted as the torch rained sparks. The girl's flanks ran with sweat.

Around she came another time. Abruptly, planting her bare feet wide apart, she wrenched her hips, her whole body, as if to drag herself to a stop again. Her arms shot out in front of her. She was so close, Dragonard had to lean back to watch.

The girl's fingertips drew the two halves of each finger cymbal together. Between each pair of little brass circles rested a small plastic sphere.

Gold eyes wide and angry, Dragonard moved. He had difficulty rising because of the men packed in close all around. The halves of the finger cymbals snicked together but this time there was no tiny ping. The cymbals cracked the hulls of the capsules the girl must have been concealing between her fingers.

From between the cymbal halves, purple smoke smelling like mustard vomited out.

Sleepgas! Dragonard thought, hauling on his rapier.

Men behind him cursed, battered at him, ordered him to sit down. Dragonard jumped up on the table behind. A grimy hand seized his boot. He kicked its owner in the head and leaped down, upsetting half a dozen spectators. Others began shouting, throwing mugs.

The purple gas boiled all around Dragonard as he kicked and elbowed his way for the door. Already his throat burned. His mind swam a little.

That sleepgas wasn't for the rest of the yelling human swine in The Sign of the Starfish; that much the quick scent of danger told him. The directions of the scar-eyed fat man, the table close by the stone floor, the gas hidden in the hands of the dancer who was darting away now—it had all been for him.

Like a lab rat down a maze tunnel, he'd been maneuvered.

Followed? Watched? *Discovered?*

It seemed certain.

By the Heart Flag?

Damn, how was it possible?

Coming from the bar, the two cowled men pulled rapiers. Another pair similarly robed broke away from a standing crowd on a kind of raised balcony at the other side of the tavern. The quartet came on through the brawling mob. Dragonard was still caught in the middle of it, finding it next to impossible to fight his way through without using his sword.

The dancer vanished through the curtain in a last tinkle of bells. The torchman slammed his brand down on the stone and rolled it with the arch of his foot, smothering it. The darkness dropped. The yelling mounted. Dragonard knew the trap had sprung full shut.

VIII

FOUR AGAINST ONE. But they'd be as blinded in the black as he was. A chance, then.

All around, bodies heaved, pushed, blundered.

" 'Ere, you damn eleyphant, off my damn boots!" a wine-stinking voice brayed close to his face. Hands twisted his elbow. "I'll give you what, stampin' all over—*raugh!*"

Breath blasted out of the unseen drunk as Dragonard hit hard, felt a suet belly indent under his fist. The hands loosed. Dragonard kicked ahead.

He had no way of knowing exactly how close his pursuers might be. A dim light oriented him as to direction. It fell from the courtyard outside, the wan flickering of lamps high up in the teetering apartments surrounding the place. A window admitted it, filthy dirty and of bottle-glass in a dark green ring pattern.

Dragonard made toward the window, turning over stools. He was carried back a yard by the seething, caterwauling mob for every two of headway.

Finally he reached the window. To his left he heard the fist-smacks and obscenities of a royal brawl. Some panicstricken guests trying to get through the shut door ahead of each other, he guessed. No use going that way.

He felt the dark with his free hand. He got hold of the leg of a stool and hoisted it to knock the bottle-glass window out.

He whipped the stool up over his head with his left arm. Wild electric pain licked into his shoulder, making him double forward with a cry.

Carrying the stool, he struck the window head first.

Eyes! his mind warned a second before the glass shattered. He twisted and dropped the stool. The force of his own involuntary dive forward carried him half over the upright shards left in the window frame. One ripped his cloak and tunic. Dragonard drove his elbows backward, striking the shards, breaking them loose. Then he dropped his free hand, caught the bottom of the frame and hauled himself outside in a sideward leap. While he was in midair, the electric pain ripped through him again, this time from his left leg. He hit the cobbles of the walled court, rolling.

Dragonard twisted on his side, scrambled up as the first of the cowled quartet leaped through the glass-toothed frame. The man's cloak belled and the cowl fell away.

The attacker's eyes were covered with immense red-lensed goggles. The rapier in his right hand glowed with a faint blue sheen at the tip.

Night goggles and stun-swords. He should have recognized the particular kind of pain that'd lanced him twice. He'd felt it first years ago, in the Academy.

Two more of the Heart Flag men leaped through the window, then the fourth. They spread into a fighting half circle. All wore the goggles that made passage in darkness no difficulty; all their sword-tips shone like blue fireflies. Dragonard held his rapier ready, backing up a step.

How they'd gotten police weapons, he couldn't imagine. Then he realized that white markets in stolen arms would probably flourish on Pentagon.

"Come along, Hastings, and no more trouble," one of them said. He put a strange, puzzling sarcasm into Dragonard's assumed name.

"A press gang, are you?" Dragonard was backing, backing toward the tunnel mouth which led under the tall apartment.

"No, just wanting a peaceable conversation. You and some friends need to get together."

Warily he backed, one step, then another.

They held their blue-tipped rapiers in front of them at half lunge position. The tavern door crashed outward and the first of the brawlers spilled into the open. They ran for the nearest wall, leaped, flung legs over, dropped out of sight. Dragonard's boots scraped the cobbles.

If he turned and ran, they'd drive the swords at his back. He wouldn't accommodate them by surrendering and going along to a night meeting with strangers. Anyway it was probably a pretext to get him off guard and into a killable position.

The goggles loomed. The hems of their black cloaks waved in the fetid wind.

"Be reasonable, Hastings. Safer for you that way."

"See you in hell first."

"Watch the sewer trough behind you, Hastings."

Trick! But the image of the slop-running stream flicked into his mind just as his left boot stepped back and down into shifting, bubbling glue.

The leader of the quartet yelled, "No more gloves with him. Swords on full stun."

Their free hands flicked over to their hilts. Switches snicked and the rapier tips brightened.

Dragonard pulled his boot out of the running garbage and stumbled across the ditch to the other side. Like a winged bird the first of the attackers jumped the sewer. Dragonard skidded around, stabbed his blade in under that of his attacker, striking for the belly.

The goggled man checked his own lunge, switched direction, drove his blade down vertically until its metal clashed and slid off Dragonard's. The contact, which Dragonard had wanted to avoid, conducted the full stun up along his right arm. Pain blasted his mind like the blow of a padded hammer.

Dragonard went crashing into the wall beside the mouth of the tenement tunnel. Now the others crossed the ditch. They converged and showed no mercy. One rapier touched his left knee cap. Dragonard's back arched in agony. A second tip hit his forearm, doubling the pain.

"We're trained as well as you ever were," the leader laughed. He slipped the point of his blade to the nape of Dragonard's neck.

The triple charge of stun beat him senseless with pain. He spun around, sword dropping from his fingers. He tried to catch the tenement wall. A nail broke as his hand dragged down across the rough stone. He struck the cobbles and rolled out, barely conscious.

Over him the swollen goggles reflected the faint light from the high apartments.

"Someone haul him up and let's get out of here."

Footfalls, like rats scurrying, clattered the tale of the tavern's patrons vanishing terrified over walls into the dark.

Two of the cloaked men lifted Dragonard.

He blacked out.

As he came back to consciousness, some fragmented images in his mind sharpened, then receded. He reflected on them without moving. They told him roughly what had happened.

He'd been laid belly down across a beast's back. He'd opened one eye and seen the beast's symmetrically scaled and armored hide stretching away from his cheek. A smell of leatheriness, a swaying, a thud of great pads sketched in the beast he never fully saw.

He had memory of a hillside. The beast had lumbered up it. At the top had been a crumbled castle, one of the old, dark, rambling ones at the far outskirts of Gannonblock.

It had loomed with jumbled towers and battlements flung at the white moons.

He was untied, driven to his feet. The goggles men clustered tightly around him, propping him up. A high keystone-arch gate full of shadows ate them. His foots dragged through the powder-dry remains of a rotted, fallen portcullis.

"Catch him!" one of the voices snarled as it all slid away. . . .

Now he woke fully.

He was seated in an old throne chair with its velveteen cushions in tatters. The chamber was vast and shadows crouched in the far corners and high nooks of the beamed ceiling. In an immense stone hearth a chemical pot burned with green flame. Its scant heat didn't reach him. The air through the slot windows high in the walls held the bite of the Pentagon outlands.

One of the goggles men, the leader, walked back and forth in front of him. His rapier tip shone a dull blue, indicating a low stun level. He noticed Dragonard awake.

"I'll say this. You live up to your reputation, Dragonard."

Inside his chest the heart muscles wrenched. He dug his hands down into the knife-scars cut deeply into the thick wooden chair arms. They knew.

They *knew*. That explained, of course, the sarcasm of the one who had pronounced the name Hastings.

He wanted to swear, leap up, attack the man. How

many might lurk around in back of him, Dragonard didn't know. He shifted cautiously, trying to see.

The leader lit a long, fragrant cigar and spun the pocket punk into the green flames of the hearth.

"You can stand up. Try and run and I'll knock you down again." The man waved the stun-sword. "For your own safety, I'll tell you that this is a very old fortress. Part of it's used as a local prison. We're not far from Gannonblock, on the edge of the desert. We have men on the towers, in the courts, all over. You might get past me. But that would be all." The man inhaled, laughing low. "Of course, it could be a good go. I'm just enough younger not to be awed all that much by your reputation. And to say you'd knocked over the great Maxdragon—well—" The younger chuckled again and puffed.

"How do you know who I am?"

"I don't know how much I'm authorized to tell you."

Dragonard's tone was contemptuous. "Use your initiative. You're high on guts with three others backing you up."

"You arrogant bastard." The goggle-lenses leaped with reflected green fire. "Well, they said you were that way."

"What's this all about?"

"Didn't we explain at the Starfish? Some old friends. A necessary conversation."

"Conversation about what?"

"On the subject of stopping you, Maxdragon, sir." Contempt was returning to him.

"Answer my first question—how you know."

The man thought, shrugged. "We've been half expecting some of the loyal old boys to try something on this order. A standing esper watch is set on every spaceport in this quadrant of II Galaxy. The espers scan every liner headed for Pentagon. They were inside your mind and out again with the true make on Hastings the moment you passed Rimmini customs."

A doorbolt squealed and went *clong* in rusty sockets. Dragonard asked, "Does this place have a name?"

"Fortress Starmarch."

On the point of asking something else, he caught his breath. The massive door swung open, and into the light of the green fire on the hearth walked a person in an ankle-length sable cloak.

From the soft litheness of the stride, Dragonard knew it was a woman. From the black kerchief bound around her upper face and hair he recognized the dancer from The Sign of the Starfish.

She halted. Her arm came free of the cloak and bells tinkled faintly under the sable folds. She unfastened the kerchief and shook out her blonde hair.

"Kristin!"

"She's one of ours," said the leader. "Boarded *Illyria Anne* at the last moment, assigned to keep you under surveillance. We don't have enough espers to send them on routine tagging missions. There could be some others slipping through at other ports to join your misguided little conspiracy. We hoped maybe she'd find out from you."

Dragonard felt gulled, furious. He said to Kristin,

"How's the munitions inventory office, dear? I wondered why you didn't show for the drink the second night. Too many lies? Guilt?"

She recoiled from his bitterness. Her blue eyes locked with his a moment, couldn't stand the anger she saw, and turned away briefly. When she faced him again, he couldn't read the stony expression of her beautiful face.

"Dragonard, I'm sorry," she said. "I didn't have a choice under the orders."

"The Heart Flag movement has some damn strange ways of recruiting."

"Fortress Starmarch is not occupied by the Heart Flag bandits. These are all my people."

The man who owned the new voice came striding into the green flame-light, his boots winking like black mirrors.

His uniform crinkled and rasped lightly. The creases were sharp and new. On his high black collar the lightning-jag emblems glowed. The man was sallow, with a pointed chin. He had the ascetic haughtiness of a saint or a professional killer or both.

Years of discipline made Dragonard straighten. He whispered the words of respect without even thinking about it: "High Commander."

"Yes," said Thomas St. Anne, High Commander of the Regulators. "But I'm afraid, Dragonard, that we may no longer be on the same side."

IX

In the stunned silence, Dragonard stared. He couldn't choose between reactions.

The sight of the High Commander brought bitterness welling up, and anger. At the same time, the powerful disciplinary training of his years at the Academy and in the Regulators hadn't faded. Regardless of the man who occupied it, the post of High Commander generated automatic respect whose manifestations were trust, awe, even hesitancy. The High Commander oversaw the activities of the police of the entire II Galaxy.

St. Anne had never been a model of manliness. His features were too small and precise. They tended to suggest craft rather than the tough physical standards of the Regulators. He wore his hair parted sharp and low on the left. Straight hair, it clung shining and tight to his round skull, like a coat of glistening fur on a ball. St. Anne drew off his gauntlets, tucked them into his belt.

"I'll have that chair, please."

His gesture sent the cowled swordsman in goggles half running. That arrogance, its answering servility, tipped the balance for Dragonard. Ugly words started to roll in his throat.

What checked them was Thomas St. Anne standing still. St. Anne recognized Dragonard's mood.

"The chair, Dragonard, is for our guest."

The High Commander executed a deferential half-turn. Kristin had already dropped to one knee, bent her head and closed her eyes. The swordsman in goggles scraped the chair as he moved it. St. Anne glared and knelt. His sharp glance indicated that Dragonard had better do the same.

Dragonard rebelled, holding his ground. He stared curiously at the burly man swinging through the great door out of the shadows, his goldleaf boots clattering in a clod's *clumph-clumph* pace.

Then Dragonard saw the pendant shaped as a radiant sun. It hung on the gold breastplate of the man with saffron skin and eyes whose corners turned upward toward his ears.

Dragonard knelt. The reflex came naturally. He imagined wild winds blowing.

"To the Lord of the Exchange," said St. Anne with downcast eyes, "greetings. Greetings and hail to His Highest Excellence, Mishubi II."

The others murmured it. Dragonard moved his lips, just to make a sound. He couldn't believe it—Mishubi II, the lord of the Tychohama systems, the heir to the electronics empire whose products were all that really linked II Galaxy together? Glancing up under his eyelids, Dragonard recognized the star king from old photofaxes he'd seen.

Mishubi II ate far too much; his belly jutted under his armor. His cape of snowy fur bore stains. The man's thick yellow arms were hairless and strong. His stump leg carried him near the hearth where he stopped. He gave Dragonard a decidedly unfriendly glance, his eyes glistened like black ball bearings. His wide face and huge spatulate nose lent him a brutish air. His age was anywhere from less than a hundred to three hundred-odd—one of the youthful Lords of the Exchange, at any rate.

"All rise, all rise." Impatiently Mishubi marched to the chair. He dropped into it with the air of one accustomed to being given the favorite place. A gold ring with the blood-red stone glistened on his right thumb. His weight made the chair creak. "You are Maxdragon?"

"Yes, Excellence."

Mishubi calculated silently. "Formidable looking fellow. The brats on the Tychohama worlds sing little songs about you. A very very famous policeman." To St. Anne, who stood near the visitor's chair as if asserting his own reflected importance: "But still with the"—Mishubi II waved his fingers near his right ear—"the tangles of the mind that make him kill?"

"Yes, Excellence," St. Anne answered. "Of course there is no technology to effect cure."

Mishubi grunted. "Of course. Now. I read your report, espers on Rimmini, your agent there—the young woman who followed him—all that I've absorbed. What else have you learned?"

"Nothing, Excellence. It's our purpose to interrogate him here in Starmarch. We only secured his person an hour ago."

"By force," Dragonard put in. "If you'd had decency to tell me—"

"You'll speak when we address you," St. Anne interrupted in turn.

Mishubi II waved. "No, let's hear Maxdragon the famous policeman." Under the saffron lids the black ball-bearing eyes showed no emotion. But neither did they reveal stupidity.

At first, with some shock, Dragonard had assessed the young star king as little more than an oaf; he'd changed his mind quickly. The Lord of the Exchange might be arrogant as all the Lords had a right to be, but he spoke with crafty deliberation. Dragonard didn't care for the ruthless shape of his face, but could a star king's ancestry be held against him?

"Tell us what you began to say," Mishubi prodded.

"I would have cooperated if these troops of yours had told me who wanted me."

Up went Thomas St. Anne's eyebrow. "Really?"

"Yes."

"Why, pray? You're a fugitive from justice, Dragonard."

Dragonard struck quickly and for the heart. "But I'm a fugitive, I expect, for the same reason you've brought a concentration of Regulators here in what I gather is some secrecy." A gesture took in the abandoned silence of Fortress Starmarch.

St. Anne coughed delicately into his hand. "We know your jailbreak was engineered by members of the Regulators. It's true we don't yet know who was behind it."

Mishubi II swung heavily to the High Commander. "Didn't the espers pick up that information?"

"No, Lord. Dragonard did not have it in his mind on a readable level during the short time he was within range at Rimmini customs."

Mishubi II picked at his fleshy lower lip with the tip of his index finger. "Dragonard, you may safely speak the truth. Tell us why you are here."

All of Dragonard's doubts and fears dwindled. The presence of the star king lolling there in the throne chair worked its effect. Confusion, chaos might exist at the lower echelons. But here, in the presence of a Lord of the Exchange, no doubt or suspicion whatsoever could exist. Dragonard was, after all, a man of his own culture. One did not spit on the floor at the foot of a throne where a god sat breathing.

"I am under secret mission orders," he said.

"Whose?" St. Anne asked.

"A member of the Regulators who is concerned with what's happening in II Galaxy."

"And precisely," said Mishubi in a murmurous voice, "what is that? Do you know?"

Dragonard's gold eyes never blinked. "The Lords of the Exchange are dying."

After a moment Mishubi turned to stare into the green chemical fire on the hearth. Dragonard caught Kristin watching him. Were those tears?

His heart hardened.

Somehow she was the one he couldn't forgive. He faced away from her. Mishubi gathered his cloak of white fur around his knees as though he were cold.

"It's true," he said. Mishubi raised his eyes. By its very passivity his look was a more dreadful warning than any Dragonard had ever experienced before. "A few know this, a very few. Some are gathered here. The rest occupy extremely high administrative posts within the Regulators. Beyond that, there is silence. The silence shall remain."

"Does anyone know why it's happening?" Dragonard asked.

He received no answer. St. Anne pulled his gloves from his belt and began to pace. He hit the gloves lightly against his leg. Mishubi scowled at the man's impatience.

"You were sent here to investigate a possible cause of the—ah—malady which is striking down the Lords, is that it?" St. Anne asked.

"Not sent," Dragonard corrected. "Asked."

"Any terms? Promises? Agreements? Rewards offered?"

How much should he tell them?

Dragonard realized that he would eventually have to tell them everything. And he suspected these men were as frightened as Sectioner Jonas Valk, though reacting in a different way. Caution seemed less and less necessary. Less desirable, too. The presence of Mishubi II and even of St. Anne, in a curious way, reassured him.

"I was promised amnesty if I succeeded."

"Succeeded in what?" St. Anne asked immediately.

"In discovering what the Heart Flag movement that's rising in the North Wastes is all about; whether it's responsible for the deaths; and if so, how."

"And to do this, you were freed illegally. By one of my own." St. Anne shook his head.

"High Commander," Dragonard said, "there was only crime in breaking the letter of the law, not the spirit. The jailbreak took place because your own people, the Regulators who know what's happened, are frightened. They've received no orders. They don't want to stand by idly while some kind of strange death threatens the men who hold II Galaxy together."

There was passion in Dragonard's voice now.

"You may not approve of what was done. It was unauthorized and illegal, admittedly. But it was done out of loyalty, not treachery. I thought we were at odds when I was manhandled up here; I don't think so now. I can see why you'd suspect me. I hope my explanation's cleared up your suspicions. I can carry out the same assignment for you that I'm carrying out for Jonas Valk, because we're on the same side after—"

In his throat Dragonard felt pain.

Their faces had changed.

Only Kristin seemed uncertain, uncomprehending. St. Anne slapped his gloves hard against his thigh.

"Ah, there it is, Sectioner Valk."

"I know his name and reputation," said Mishubi, rising. "Admirable loyalty."

And then Dragonard saw the laughing cruelty under the saffron lids.

St. Anne spoke to the leader of the swordsmen. "Wheel in the view console, please. I want to make certain this is done swiftly and properly." The leader dashed out. St. Anne said to Dragonard, "I rather had a notion it might be old Jonas. But it could have been a number of others. We have police assassinators in position at several of the likeliest locations, carrying assassin report cameras. One is stationed just outside the h.q. where Valk is now working and living on Questro Blue, evidently awaiting your report."

"Assassinators?" Dragonard almost choked on the word. "You sound as though you don't want to find out what the Heart Flag is trying—"

"We don't," said Mishubi II.

"A slight amendment, Lord?" St. Anne asked. Mishubi II shrugged to give leave. "Let us put it this way, Dragonard. We want the investigation to proceed no further."

"You don't want to know what's killing the star kings?" Dragonard yelled.

"We've all said quite enough," Mishubi grunted.

For the first time in long minutes, Kristin spoke. Her voice shook. "High Commander, I didn't know there would be assassins—"

"Your rank doesn't merit your knowing." Coldly St. Anne turned his back.

The leader of the swordsman rolled in a cylindrical unit of gleaming metal. St. Anne touched a control and the front half of the cylinder revolved out of the way. A talk wand popped out of a socket and hovered in the air alongside an oversized viewing screen. St. Anne took the wand and pressed its tip. Purple and pink sequencing lights lit the board below the screen.

"I want the station assigned to Sectioner Valk, please," St. Anne said into the wand.

A wheezing, a thrumming. Then a filtered, sexless voice replied, "Station Omicron standing by, High Commander."

"Kill him," said St. Anne. "And light up so we can watch."

The screen zigzagged with scanner lines. A chromatically bright image flopped into view. Dragonard saw an institutionally bare corridor like those in police barracks all over the galaxy. The image came toward the viewers, as in a dolly shot. It joggled. An assassin report camera was customarily carried in a plastic ring which the police hireling wore around his neck.

Pardoned habitual criminals with little more than vegetables for minds, the assassins were employed by the Regulators only when highest policy dictated removal of, say, an influential and otherwise untouchable criminal. Dragonard had grown up believing the system to be accepted, but had never been on a case where an assassin had to be employed.

"The man's cursedly slow," Mishubi complained.

"But efficient, Excellence. Omicron does his work well," St. Anne replied.

Wind crooned and sang through the emptiness of Fortress Starmarch. On the screen a gloved hand reached out through the dimness of the barracks hall at dead of night. The apartment door was unlocked. The screen image dulled behind a patina of dark red as the assassin switched to his night goggles.

And Dragonard began to smell the stink of conspiracy blowing in Pentagon's night wind.

Horror-struck, he stared from face to face.

Mishubi watched, interested.

St. Anne tensed forward, concerned.

Only Kristin revealed raw emotion—bafflement, fright. A glance she flashed him was poignant, disturbed, as if saying, *I don't know anything about this! Not anything!*

The assassin's hands appeared at the screen's lower edge, reaching.

Omicron struck quickly. The camera in his throat-ring rushed in as he leaped. For a terrible second Jonas Valk's face filled the screen like a deep scarlet balloon. His moustache twitched, then his eyes rolled as the surprise and terror of death and biting hands registered.

With a scream Dragonard started forward. *"God damn it, don't kill him–"*

The leader with the stun-sword darted in front of him, rapier tip blue again. Dragonard ran into the tip. His throat touched it and jolting pain drove him back.

On the screen Omicron strangled Jonas Valk,

shook him several times and then flung him like so many rags down on his disturbed bedclothes.

"Well done," said St. Anne. He switched off and thrust the wand into its socket as the screen blacked out.

Staggering from the sword's bite, Dragonard rubbed his throat and tried to fathom it. He couldn't. Mishubi II a traitor to the very confederation of Lords to which he belonged? St. Anne slaughtering his own kind? The implications and the reasons eluded Dragonard's beaten mind. But like a ripping knife, the knowledge of what he himself had done did not.

They had been serious all along, tracking him, kidnapping him.

They wanted a loyal Sectioner's investigator stopped.

In the name of all howling, senseless infinity—why?

He'd believed them, trusted them, invested them with goodness and sincerity they didn't possess. He saw it stripped away now, in Mishubi's calculating gaze, St. Anne's sweaty forehead and look of relief.

"Stop staring," St. Anne said. "You'll never understand it because we don't intend that you understand it. The Heart Flag movement is of no importance. Your mission is canceled. You told us what we want to know. Thank you."

"My mission is not canceled," Dragonard shouted. "I killed Jonas, telling you. God knows what's going on here, but I'll find out—"

The leader bawled for his swordsmen, who jumped to block Dragonard's charge.

Kristin cried out, her hands over her face. St. Anne's composure broke. The stun-swordsmen swarmed around Dragonard and jabbed him with blow after charged blow. He dropped to his knees. St. Anne closed his fist at his sides and shrieked like a hysterical woman.

"The mission is canceled! You'll go nowhere except into a cell until we put you under a psychic depth probe and find out what else you know!"

Killed him, Dragonard thought, swinging with bare fists. Jonas—*I killed him.*

They stunned him, lugged him down three flights and locked him in a cell without lights.

X

LATE THAT NIGHT Kristin came to the cell.

Dragonard heard her identify herself to the guard using her police rank number. The number told him that she had graduated from the Woman's Academy three years ago, and had been promoted two grades in the Regulators since.

Old rust-flaked hinges squealed. Kristin's supple body glowed with a pearly radiance as she came in. She'd exchanged her cloak and dancer's costume for a plain gray drill uniform and half-boots with no rank patches or other decoration. The severe cut of the field blouse and trousers concealed some of the richness of her figure.

Yet Dragonard was cuttingly aware of her beauty and that angered him. He glowered.

She pushed the great metal door shut. Its tarnished bronze hinge straps shone a sickly green in the pale softness emanating from the four inch light wand clipped to her black leather belt.

Her blue eyes held his in silence. She was unusually pale. She'd wiped away all her makeup, brushed her hair back and caught it at the nape of her neck with a regulation ring of gray steel.

"Time for the depth probe already, dear?" he asked. Mockery danced in his long gold eyes. He was haggard. "Or some other reason? They certainly wouldn't send you out of consideration for my creature comforts. So it must be the other way around."

"Please, Dragonard—"

"They sent you to rub my nose in it."

"Don't talk that way. Don't."

"To remind me of how I wrapped my teeth all the way around the bait."

"Mishubi and St. Anne are having a dinner in private. They don't know I'm here."

"Excuse me if I think you're lying."

"Oh, God. I don't blame you for feeling that way."

"At least I communicate my mood. They'll need more than a girl to get me to the probe equipment. Go back and tell them to send a squad. Men ready to bleed."

Kristin shuddered, her breasts lifting out a moment in relief under the dull gray tunic. "No wonder suspects used to be afraid of you. Sometimes your face looks as though human life doesn't matter at all."

Dragonard lifted a boot, set it on the stone outcrop which served as the cell's bed. He hunched, elbows resting on his bent knee. "And the price keeps declining. Even the lives of the Lords don't seem to matter much. What the hell are you people doing? What kind of a filthy plan do you have?"

Angrily Kristin shook her head. "I was wrong to come here."

"Yes, if you expected I'd trust you."

"I don't know *what* they're planning!" she burst out. In the corners of her eyes moisture gathered like little diamonds. "Call that a lie too but I'm only following orders. I have no idea why Mishubi is here. I only know it's a secret."

What damn emotion was tricking him now? He half believed her. Self-protection darted a new thought into his mind. He made a circular gesture with his right hand, mouthing the words in silence: "Is this place bugged?"

"No. I checked the guard commander's equipment upstairs just to be sure. I felt Starmarch wouldn't be. Didn't St. Anne mention it? This is a very old civil prison. In the next wing there are regular prisoners locked up right now, a dozen or more in every one of a whole series of common cells. Every wall in Starmarch is two feet thick, too. And the High Commander hasn't been here long enough to have listeners built in."

"How long has he been here?"

"His ship arrived an hour ahead of *Illyria Anne*."

"Was the Lord with him?"

"Mishubi came in an unmarked cruiser. A skysled landed him in the desert to the north. I'm trying to tell you, Dragonard—that I don't know *what's* happening. I had no idea that the High Commander was trying to trick you into revealing the Sectioner's name."

Deeper and more sullen gold his eyes shone now. "Valk was a fine man."

"Understand—I didn't know he'd be killed. It sickened me as much as it did you."

The unbidden belief overwhelmed him. Suspicion cautioned him. "Why should I think you're telling the truth now? You lied like hell on the ship."

"That was my job." Kristin gave a forlorn little shrug. "I didn't think I could convince you."

"Why did you bother to come?"

Her head lifted. Her cheeks had reddened from tears. "You do things because you must. I had to come down here and tell you I didn't know about the murder."

A knot inside him loosened a little. He took her shoulders. "If that's not just one more lie, you're taking a horrible risk."

"Even so, I—had to do it."

"The second night on *Illyria Anne*, you never showed up for the drink."

"I had a job and that's all when they assigned me to board and check up on your destination. But after I met you there were"—a hoarseness in her voice as she pulled away, turned so that she faced the cell door—"personal reasons why I didn't want to get any more involved with you. I found out enough the first night to report via longwave. And one encounter was enough. You're—well, maybe not the animal they make you out to be. But you're—Mishubi expressed it—formidable."

She faced him again. Her cheeks showed a redness that had nothing to do with tears. "I think I've said enough to make it clear. Don't humiliate me by more questions."

Touched, Dragonard barely breathed. "No. I won't."

Inside, he was all heat and aching. *Careful!*

He didn't listen. He wanted to take her in his arms and kiss her. She folded her arms quickly.

The tension broke.

"All right," he said. "Let's grant you knew nothing about Valk's murder ahead of time."

"I swear, Ma—Dragonard. I swear that's true."

"Did you know the Regulators broke me out of the prison on Rankor?"

"My superior told me that much before I boarded *Illyria Anne*. And I knew the wind was blowing something awfully big when he also said I'd report personally to the High Commander when I arrived."

"But you weren't told which Regulator was responsible for breaking me."

"No, I wasn't. They acted as if he knew. I was told that catching you was what mattered. Catching you and preventing you from making contact with this rebel army that calls itself the Heart Flag."

Dragonard scratched his chin. "What do you know about the Heart Flag movement?"

"Very little. It's attracting the scum. They disappear into the North Wastes but I don't have any idea why."

"How about St. Anne? Does he know?"

"I'm not sure. I thought he didn't. But then he pretended to know about Valk, didn't he?" She moved nearer, as if the tangible warmth of her would help convince him. "I thought I was being loyal to the force, that's all. Helping to catch an escaped criminal and abort some kind of unauthorized mission. When I met the High Commander just before we set the trap at the inn, St. Anne mentioned you and used the word treason."

The word hung heavy in the air. Finally Dragonard's shoulders lifted a little. Some kind of twisted sense was emerging. He saw only the surface of it, not the reasons lying festered underneath. But the surface had pattern and order at last.

"If there's treason, Kristin, the traitor must be St. Anne."

"It couldn't be. Mishubi II is one of the Lords."

"I know. That part I don't understand yet. Maybe St. Anne is tricking him too. I don't know why he would, but I know the answer's out there." Dragonard's eyes swung to the cell's wall. He never lost his sense of direction. "In the North Wastes where the Heart Flag army's gathering. I—"

Kristin waited for him to finish. He didn't because he was still not entirely sure of her.

He wanted to be sure, as he had seldom wanted anything else. Yet caution prodded him to keep his decision silent—the decision to penetrate the North Wastes and complete the mission.

That way and only that way could he hope to discover what treason the High Commander of the Regulators was plotting against the dying star kings. That way, too, he could give a memorial to the man who'd befriended him long ago, tried to save him from humiliation and prison, then given him a second chance. He thought of Valk's kindly leathery face and dragoon moustache a last time, then put the Sectioner from his mind.

Kristin saw the change that had come over him. He almost smiled.

"I must go," she said.

"Yes, all right. Thanks for coming."

"You believe me? What I told you?"

Should he test her now? Ask for her help?

No, too soon. Other alternatives remained to be explored.

St. Anne's next move, for instance, might reveal some useful information. There was also the possibility of demanding an audience with Mishubi II, though that seemed unlikely to be of much value. If it came to a test of stories, the High Commander's word would carry weight while his would carry little or none at all. Besides, he didn't know the nature of St. Anne's plot yet, or why it was so crucially important that the Heart Flag be left alone by the Regulators.

So Dragonard touched her face and said, "Yes, I believe you."

"I'll try to find out what they're going to do with you."

"St. Anne mentioned depth probe."

"Yes, but I have no idea when. I'll try to come back and let you know."

Treason there too? Treason in those blue eyes that held his, hurting and full of some emotion he would nearly have given his life to hear her speak aloud?

Was that light real? Or was it put there only by what was inside of him, a self-deception? She could still be spying and intriguing for Thomas St. Anne. He mustn't forget.

"I hope I'm still alive when you get back with the news," he said.

"Oh, God." She sobbed it very softly, pulled the door open and fled.

Dragonard felt exhilarated. On the surface the situation seemed hopeless, yet now he had the awful, vengeful drive to keep pushing on, and it was like being drunk. He ran his hands over the north wall, as if he were trying to see through it to the empty deserts of Pentagon running north beyond it, north and north and north under the three white moons.

The North Wastes. He must get into the North Wastes.

An hour later a guard squad removed him from the cell and marched him to the next wing. He was thrown into one of the common cells with a batch of other prisoners.

As the iron gates of the pen shut behind him, Dragonard wondered whether he'd been put in with the others so that a stabbing or a beating could be arranged. The underworld still reached prisoners that way, paying someone already locked up to get next to a prisoner and kill him on some pretext. A man who had sold out the Regulators could use the same gambit. Maybe St. Anne's threat of a psychic depth probe was so much smokescreen.

Face impassive, Dragonard looked from man to man in the sour, straw-strewn room of rock. One chemical torch in a niche shed feeble blue light. A high barred window let in the night's moon-brilliance and the silhouette of an armed man on a stone rampart. The prisoners lay about in stupefied indifference. Dragonard saw bleary, brutalized eyes, chins filthy with stubble, clothes in tatters.

No one so much as grunted.

Which one, Dragonard wondered, had St. Anne hired to finish him?

XI

"THERE'S SOME clean straw over here if you want to sit down," someone said.

The speaker was sprawled in the dimmest corner of the room, so still he almost appeared to be part of the shadows. Dragonard walked over, past a low, round platform of wood with stone legs. On this platform were three shallow pans: two contained a gray gruel; the third was half full of pink liquid. A chain about three feet long fastened each pan to the wood.

The prisoner in the corner shifted to the right in the straw and Dragonard squatted down.

"Thanks."

"Extending the full facilities of the house is the least I can do. Especially since our hosts don't go out of their way to provide a welcome."

The prisoner's speech was as merrily mocking as his face. Hardly more than twenty, the young man wore several layers of tunics and cloaks, some with colorful patches and all of them in shreds.

The boy-man had a pleasantly vulpine face. He appeared to be native to Pentagon. On his right wrist shone a bronze bracelet displaying the interlocked rings of Pentagon. Worn hide-and-thong sandals on his feet completed the costume. His black hair hung to his shoulders in the style of the North Waste men but his nose was narrow and hawkish, rather than flat. Over his right eye hung a scrap of leather held in place by a head-string. His good eye was bright blue, intelligent and faintly amused. Dragonard took him for a beggar. At least he'd seen a few in similar attire around Gannonblock.

"You'll get used to the stink after a while," the prisoner said. "It's not bad now. Sometimes they toss stim drunks in with us and they vomit."

"Pleasant thought." Dragonard was purposely inane, guarded.

"I'm sure the Lords don't smell such elegant stinks in their fine palaces, though."

"The Lords of the Exchange?"

The young man laughed. "I don't know any other Lords, do you? Silk sheets and forty doctors hovering and never a thought to dungholes like this. Ah, it must be splendid."

"I wouldn't know."

"Keep your mouth shut over there so some of us can sleep," came a growl.

Dragonard turned. The complainer had risen up on the far side of the common cell, an obese man in a frayed leather uniform. Threads and rips showed where official patches had been torn away. The man's huge bald head gleamed blue in the glow of the chemical torch in the niche above him. A webbing of red scars covered his right cheek.

"Yes, sir, Officer," said the beggar-boy with a contemptuous salute.

"And watch your slobbering mouth or I'll fix it for you, hear me?"

"Of course, Officer. I tremble. I shiver. I invite you to try."

The beggar-boy's good blue eye glared like ice and mockery no longer danced in his tone. He shifted slightly forward on the straw. The fat man saw the challenge of the white, humorless, defiant grin. With an oath he rolled over on his side, turning away. As he lowered his bald head he glanced quickly at Dragonard, then fleshy lids dropped shut. The man appeared to sleep.

A coldness walked up Dragonard's backbone. The fat man had seemed curious about him.

Better watch. He might be the one.

"Damn hog of a bully," the beggar-boy muttered to Dragonard. "Been in here only six hours and he's broken one man's arm already. Just because the man stumbled against him."

"He looks like he's been stripped of his rank, whatever it was."

"Local revenue collector. Caught with his fingers in the credit machine."

An official. The kind St. Anne would select, offering freedom. Dragonard knew how that worked, all right.

"I'd like a go at him," the beggar-boy said, picking at a tooth with a straw.

Instantly Dragonard liked his companion. The beggar-boy's courage was quiet, held no boastfulness. The young man added, "My name is Jeremy Lynx."

Still being careful, Dragonard replied with a grunt of acknowledgment.

"What's the reason for your lockup?" Jeremy asked.

"I don't know. They haven't read the charges yet."

The tooth-picking straw went flying, thrown. "That's typical of the way the Lords operate these days."

"I get the impression you haven't much feeling for them."

"Why, you're a clever fellow, whatever-your-name-is. I never knew my dislike showed; I thought everyone believed I loved the Lords the way a stupid child loves a father who beats it with a belt whenever it yells for food. I must control my tongue. The authorities won't like me."

Laughing, Jeremy Lynx hunched up to a sitting position. His gaze slid off Dragonard's. He'd been trying for a reaction but Dragonard's face remained unchanged. Jeremy pointed.

"That pink swill on the stool is vitamin supplement. Once a day we get a bowl of it. It's decomposed but if you can stand the smell, it'll keep you going. Don't touch the gruel. Worms."

Nodding, Dragonard rose. He hadn't had anything to drink in a while. His throat was dry.

As he reached the stool the fat man sat up, straw falling off his shoulders.

"Leave that," the fat man said.

Dragonard's hand hung in the air, halfway to the bowl. "It's all yours, is it?"

"They portion it according to how many's in here. They didn't count you when they poured that bowl. You're not entitled to any."

"For God's sake," Jeremy yelled out of the dark. "Act human for a change, hog-head. You see how much is left. We aren't exactly fighting over it."

The fat man's pink lips twitched. He breathed heavily as he shoved himself up and stood. All over the cell, prisoners shifted, rustling the straw. Eyes blinked, heads raised.

The fat man brushed straw off his leather uniform. His nose shone with sweat as he walked forward. He went past Dragonard, speaking to Jeremy, who was rising out of the corner.

"I've listened to your puking smart tongue long enough tonight."

"Go to hell and let me sleep."

"You're high and mighty for a beggar. You talk, talk, talk—and think you can get away with it."

Several of the prisoners growled warnings. They urged the fat man to go back to his place, avoid trouble. Dragonard watched, gold eyes bright. Jeremy Lynx was backed into the corner; he didn't seem especially troubled. He arranged the hanging tatters of his cloaks and tunics as though they were fine garments.

"Do you want to sit down again?" Jeremy asked, studying a speck on his filthy outer cloak. "Or do you want me to crack your dirty unwashed neck for you?" He raised his head and smiled. His blue eye shone as he snapped out the finish of it. "Answer your betters, hog-head."

Screaming, the fat man smashed the beggar-boy's groin with his knees.

Jeremy tried for a punch but couldn't get it off. He doubled over. The fat man seized the back of his neck and wrenched.

With an outrush of breath the beggar-boy tumbled. The fat man kicked his head against the wall and Jeremy let out one low yelp of pain.

Dragonard went striding for the corner. He caught a leather shoulder, pulled hard.

"Leave him alone. He's a third your weight."

The suet face split open, happily grinning. "But you're not."

Up came fat hands at fantastic speed. Dragonard's instincts started him backward, not quite in time. The fat man's thumbs struck at his eyes, quick jabs bringing multicolored blindness.

Dragonard staggered. He couldn't see. But the swine grin on the fat man's face had told him enough—the fat man was eager to fight. *This is the one St. Anne sent.*

Dragonard stumbled against the round wooden platform, blinking furiously. "He's behind you," Jeremy called from the shooting star confusion that was all Dragonard saw. A chopping pain signaled a blow delivered to Dragonard's neck. He nearly went down. He grabbed the pan of vitamin fluid and hit with it, but the chain didn't reach. The fat man caught his wrist with both hands, bent and bit down to the bone like an animal.

Dragonard felt blood run. Some of his sight came back. The fat man's face filled his vision, distorted, sweatingly happy.

And the redness rushed in like sea-combers from the corners of his mind.

His hands shot at the fat neck. The other man's power was considerable. He struck at Dragonard's head, shoulders, belly. Dragonard panted, holding on. He hauled the fat man from side to side as the prisoners screeched and applauded.

The fat man drove punches, kicks into Dragonard's stomach and genitals. The hurt made his mind redden all the more. With his left leg he tripped the fat man, caught him as he fell and dropped on top of him with both knees.

Squealing, the fat man dragged his nails down Dragonard's face. Then he went for the eyes again with his thumbs, Dragonard twisted his head out of the way. Everything turned bright red.

He felt the metal vitamin pan in his hands, the chain clinking. The fat man wanted to kill him. His blood raced.

Smashed it down.

Smashed it down.

Smashed.

Smashed.

He was going under. Control was gone, just as at other times in the past. He wanted to stop and couldn't. The fat man wasn't struggling hard any longer. But Dragonard's mind was lit like a red furnace.

Down came the bloodied basin.

Down again.

Down again.

Everything turned white-crimson.

His head ached. The walls of the common cell swam, shifting like jelly. Dragonard's belly hurt. He opened his eyes all the way.

Jeremy Lynx hunched down in front of him. Like specters, the other prisoners huddled in small groups off in the blurring distance.

"The guards hauled the body out," Jeremy said.

"Did I—?"

Dragonard saw a pool of blood where the straw had been kicked aside near the wood platform. One of the chains had been sawed through but the bowls remained. He pinched the top of his nose.

"Yes. You said body. God." Dragonard's belly hurt with defeat.

"I owe you my life, my friend," Jeremy said softly. His blue eye was oddly intense.

"No, I think he was really after me."

"I don't know what the guard will do. After they took the body they gave you an injection. You've been sleeping for several hours." Jeremy bobbed his head toward the high window, where morning redness thrust in. He continued, "I wondered how a man could fight as savagely as you did. But while you were out, you talked some." He paused. "Dragonard."

Wedged into the corner and sitting awkwardly on the base of his spine with his legs shot out in front of him, Dragonard knew deep panic.

Jeremy pushed at his shoulder, easing him back.

"The rest don't know. They're too stupid to care. Ordinary criminals."

"And you?" Dragonard's eyes sharpened. "Not so ordinary?"

A shrug pushed the question aside. "You cursed and yelled in your sleep. I asked some questions. You gave me your real name—Dragonard. Everyone's heard of the cashiered policeman with the red hands. I understood. At least I understood who you were. Why you fought the way you did and killed him that way."

"What other questions did you ask?"

Jeremy smiled a small smile. "Just questions. You did talk about the Heart Flag."

The leather eyepatch contrasted with the inquiring blue eye. Dragonard saw symbolism there: the patch for the beggar personality Jeremy affected; the blue eye for what lay hidden. And Jeremy no longer looked as youthful. He had aged without adding years. Dragonard's head ached less now. He felt like a gamble, and tried it.

"There's not too much of a secret to it. I was sent here to investigate the Heart Flag. I was locked up to prevent that investigation."

The blue eye widened. "Locked up by your own?"

"Yes. By the Regulators. I was sprung from prison by another Regulator, secretly."

"The Regulators don't want you to find out about the Heart Flag?"

"One Regulator doesn't. The High Commander."

Jeremy Lynx said, "Policeman, I had a feeling we had plenty in common."

"Do we?"

"Maybe more than you know. I have a certain interest in the Heart Flag, because—"

A clatter of boots outside the iron gates silenced him.

Guards rolled one set of gates aside while other guards stood back, pointing blasters. One guard crossed the straw and motioned Dragonard up.

Jeremy Lynx seemed to shrink, turn small, head bent in fear and subservience, a clever screen.

Dragonard didn't resist. He was prodded to the corridor and down to a small, heated room at the end of the long row of common cells. The door clanged. Dragonard found himself alone with a desk-top communicator such as a captain of the watch would use.

The screen zigzagged, sharpened, and Thomas St. Anne appeared against a neutral background.

"Any feelings of repentance, Dragonard? Any desire to cooperate?"

"Sorry, the cell hasn't had that effect."

"Pity."

"You don't really mean that, High Commander."

"I fail to understand you."

"Come off it. Your thug tried to kill me and failed. Try something else."

On the screen Thomas St. Anne's face briefly acknowledged the truth of Dragonard's words. Then the High Commander became impassive again. He sighed.

"Not until tomorrow. Several matters of importance will keep me busy all day. We won't be able to depth probe you for at least twenty-four hours." St. Anne's eyes looked out of the screen, direct and pitiless. "Of course you won't be much good to anyone after that."

Dragonard chuckled. "And I probably won't even be strong enough to live through it, is what you mean. What if I did cooperate, High Commander? What if I apologized? Would you send me back to Rankor?"

"Of course not," said St. Anne. "Rest well today."

Amused, he reached for a control that wiped the screen dark.

The guards ushered Dragonard back. It was clear there was no way out except the way Dragonard might make himself—an escape. Otherwise, he'd merely wait until St. Anne killed him. The depth probe was a fraud. They'd probably administer an accidental over-voltage. St. Anne wanted him out of the way for good and all. It rather came as a relief to know what had to be done.

The next question was—how?

Kristin came to the cell after nightfall. She wore cloak and cowl and carried her light-wand. Dragonard met her at the bars.

The outer corridor stretched empty either way. Evidently she'd used her authority to clear it. Down the cell row somewhere, two prisoners argued in whining monotones. Water trickled through the sewage run in the center of the stone floor behind her.

Dragonard reached through the bars to touch her hand. She closed her fingers, warm. Her cheeks were red and puffed.

"The depth probe—" she began.

"I already know," he said under his breath. "Tomorrow. They're going to kill me."

"If we could just talk alone somewhere—"

Dragonard jerked his head to indicate the lumps of shadow in the cell behind. The one chemical torch had fused out at sunset and hadn't been replaced.

"Most of them are sleeping. They won't interfere anyway—they're frightened. I went berserk and killed another man last night. The only consolation is, he'd been sent to kill me first. St. Anne does want me dead." Dragonard pushed his face as close to the bars as he could. "I wish I could kiss you. It's pretty late for pretense. You wouldn't be here if you were really working for the High Commander. The pattern's coming clear finally. They don't want me to go on."

With a tiny cry she pressed her cheek to the bar. Dragonard could almost reach it with his lips. He felt faint heat in the space between them, or imagined he did.

"I wish I hadn't fallen in love with you," she said. "If we had—"

Surprise caught in her throat, making her leap back. Dragonard's neck went cold and his hands whipped up to strike whoever had crept up behind them.

Jeremy Lynx caught his wrist and held back the blow. The one blue eye gleamed.

"Is she with them or not?" he whispered.

"Who is he?" Kristin breathed.

"Friend," said Dragonard. "No, Jeremy. She's not with them any more."

Jeremy seized the bars, talked to her. "We need an ordinary scrambler that will open this door and the one to the outside. We also need a lantern. We need those things by twelve tonight. Can you get them?"

Kristin hesitated. "I don't know. I'll try."

Dragonard asked, "What happens tonight, beggar-man? If that's what you really are."

Jeremy's lips peeled back. It was no smile. "You'll have to wait to discover that. It'll be worth it to you, I think."

"Someone's coming to try to break you out," Dragonard said.

"With emphasis on the try. If this girl's on your side, she can give us a real chance. But it has to be before midnight or it won't do any good."

Dragonard's eyes slitted down. "Why should I go along back to Gannonblock with a bunch of your beggar friends?"

"Let's both stop pretending, policeman. They'll look like beggars but they'll come from the other way, north. And we'll be riding back that way too if we make it. Mine's a very simple proposition." The young man's good eye shone bright as a blue flame. "Help me to make it out and I'll lead you to the Heart Flag."

A prisoner snored in the stillness. Dragonard nodded.

He squeezed Kristin's hand hard through the bars, telling her with the touch that he loved her.

"Try for us," he said.

"All right," she answered.

"Midnight," Jeremy whispered between his teeth.

But she had already gone, cloak belling behind.

XII

STRIPES OF moonglare fell between the window bars, lighting the straw. A prisoner sleeping propped against the round wood platform sobbed in a nightmare. Nothing else stirred.

Dragonard hadn't slept at all. He feigned it, sitting uncomfortably in one black corner of the cell. Jeremy Lynx sat nearby with his legs stuck straight out. Every half minute or so Jeremy shifted. He laid his right ankle on top of his left, then he moved his left on top. Before long he had his right on top again. The changing of position got on Dragonard's nerves.

"Stop that damn jumping around."

"I'm worried. Are you sure you can trust that girl?"

"I'd say the time's past for worrying." Under his closed eyelids Dragonard saw her painfully lovely face. Would he see her again after tonight? Ever? "She'll come."

"But it's midnight."

Jeremy pushed himself up straighter with his palms. He rose and padded to the center of the cell. The light of the three high-wheeling moons crisscrossed his grimy sandaled ankles and turned them silver. He lifted his face toward the window and shut his eyes, listening. His eyepatch blazed like burnished metal. Then he walked back and squatted down.

"Midnight on the dot," he said.

"No, I've got an internal clock. And I know that desert out there. The wind shifts right at twelve this time of year. Comes blowing in from the North Wastes. Listen. Hear?"

Sure enough, Dragonard's ears picked up a subtle, keening whine, a rushing moan that was new.

Jeremy cursed half aloud. "Either she can't find what we need, which I doubt—she's a member of the Regulators, after all, and that gives her the run of Starmarch—or she's trotted back to tell the ones on top and they'll tease us a while, then come for us. Or maybe she *could* make it but she's too frightened and won't risk the consequences. Considering she's a woman, I'll take the last choice. Damn. If it had been a man we could trust, he'd 've had the guts to—"

"She'll be here," Dragonard interrupted.

But doubt's little teeth chewed his nerves.

Silence.

Dragonard's palms sweated. Outside the cell, a distant lamp cast a motionless, elongated guard's shadow down the corridor ceiling. Dragonard strained for some sound of Kristin approaching. All he heard was a faint rumbling as of a rainstorm many miles away.

On Pentagon rainfall was negligible.

Jeremy caught the drumming.

"That's it. They're here. I wanted to signal them from a wall. Now they'll have to ax us out, if they can get this far inside and *if* we can yell loudly enough so they know where we are."

Once again Jeremy cursed. Hours ago, he'd ceased to resemble a beggar-boy. Layers of dissembling peeled away invisibly. Now all Dragonard saw was a tense, moon-flooded face. The face of a man. A warrior . . . hard . . . purposeful . . . embittered by frustration.

"Who's out there?" Dragonard asked.

"Men who'll have to do your ladyfriend's work for us now that—"

Jeremy's last words blended into an abrupt, thudding explosion that shook all Starmarch.

"Bless her, Bel brought the bombard," Jeremy said. "It's half a hundred years old, and the damn thing threatens to blow up all the time. The airlift must be working again—"

Another gigantic thud slammed the night and men stirred in the cell. One whimpered. Two sat up and began asking obscene questions about what was happening. Once before Dragonard had heard a sound like the one ripping the night. On a parade ground years ago, a sonic bombard was dragged out of storage at a Regulators' barracks for a review by visiting brass. The ancient weapon blew itself apart on the first pull of the lanyard.

The thuds repeated, one falling on top of another. A gradual tide of noise rose within the Fortress: a siren wailed up and down the scale; ray rifles hissed and lit the blackness outside the cell window; boots hammered; riding-beasts stamped in their pens, pulled on their tethers, bleated their fear; orders hallooed from post to post.

Out in the desert the rhythmic beating of the bombard continued. Somewhere nearer, stone collapsed in a roar.

"Let me stand on your shoulders," Jeremy said. "I'll yell. Maybe they can locate us that way."

Dragonard twisted, staring into the corridor beyond the bars. All shadows of guards had disappeared. The siren echoed through a nearby amplifier. Jeremy must be right; she wasn't coming.

Bitterly he spun back to the window and cupped his interlaced hands. Jeremy shoved a prisoner aside and stepped into Dragonard's hands with his right sandal.

A clicking in the corridor.

"Wait."

Dragonard lunged to the bars again.

From the direction of the lighted guard post the shadow of a running figure leaped out along the ceiling. A last guard bolted from the room where Dragonard had confronted St. Anne on the screen earlier. Still cloak-muffled, Kristin rushed past the man. He was going the other way. The bombard roared and the guard never glanced around.

She reached the bars but did not throw back her cowl. Dragonard slid his fingers through. As she pressed the scrambler into his fingers she whispered, "I've been waiting in the bend of the hall almost an hour. This light was too big to carry past the guards. I began to think I'd never be able to make it. Then that noise started."

"My apologies," Jeremy laughed. "I doubted you. Got the lock?"

"Not quite yet." Dragonard maneuvered the scrambler into position and pressed the trigger.

Prisoners rushed at them from behind. One squealed, "What's happening? Is it an escape?"

"Take your hands off me." Jeremy's fist felled the man. "Fend for yourselves. Hurry up, Dragonard. I can't keep these jackals off forever—"

Now the cry growled or sang from all the convicts' throats in the cell.

"It's an escape!"

"We're under attack!"

"Kill the bastards if they won't take us!"

"Knock blind-eyes out of the way!"

Hysterically the men surged at Jeremy. He shielded Dragonard, who was bent over the lock waiting for the mechanism to release. The metal cube was slippery in Dragonard's fingers and he nearly dropped it.

Thirty seconds ran out.

Forty-five. Dragonard was hurled against the bars as the prisoners beat at Jeremy Lynx from all sides. Jeremy fought like a professional. He used hands, feet, teeth to beat and bite them back.

The thuds of the bombard shook the whole Fortress. Men's voices and the firing of ray rifles rose to a din. Finally the lock gave.

Dragonard pitched through the doorway, whirled, caught Jeremy and held him upright to keep him from falling into the slop-runnel. Kristin's cowl fell away as she ran forward to hand him an old, rusting ring-top lantern.

"I hope the chem cell has fuel left," she said. "There was no time to check."

Dragonard yanked her cowl up over her blonde hair to hide her face. None of the prisoners racing out of the cell paid attention. But in the other common cells, men still imprisoned hung on the bars and howled. If one saw Kristin's face and later reported her—

"Farewell time was hours ago," Jeremy said to him. "Are you coming?"

"Make sure they see you somewhere else, Kristin," Dragonard breathed. The lantern weighted his right hand. He wrapped his left around her for a tearing second, jerking her body against his. He pressed his face under her cowl. He felt her lips on his skin, and the coolness of her tears. She murmured his name.

No more time.

He tore away and followed Jeremy Lynx down the corridor, running hard.

Most of the freed prisoners had no idea of directions. They plunged every-which-way down tunnels at a dimly lit branching. Jeremy, on the other hand, went more slowly, moving with clear purpose and direction. The tunnel he chose ran straight ahead from the junction. Blackness swallowed the two of them.

"Hold up," Jeremy whispered in the chill, dank air. "I'm feeling for an opening—ah. The wall on your right. I'll go first."

Dragonard's feet found ancient steps, worn concave through the centuries. These led straight up in the dark. Dragonard counted fifty steps, fifty more. The bombard thundered far away. Thick stone walls muffled all sound.

"Turning left," Jeremy called. "Light ahead. We'll be on the ramparts in a minute."

The steps continued upward, a dozen more of them. Then the whiteness of the three moons washed a stone passage which ran dead level for a short distance before it opened onto a red-glaring night. A Regulator with a ray rifle ran past the opening, then another.

"Get the lantern going," Jeremy ordered.

The turn-key refused to turn even under the pressure of Dragonard's strong fingers. He bit his teeth together and grunted. It moved a fraction.

He applied more pressure. The outer flange of the key cut deep into his thumb-ball, smearing his fingers with blood. He ignored the pain and kept turning.

At the heart of the lantern a phosphorescent white spot appeared and grew like a blurry jewel behind the frosted plates of the six-sided light. Jeremy reached the tunnel's entrance. Dragonard crowded up behind him. A few yards ahead, the serrated battlement of Fortress Starmarch spread left and right, the wall dropping straight away in front of it. This was the side of the fortress facing away from Gannonblock. Out there under the harsh glare of the moons spread a drifting, sandy waste with outcroppings of basalt for a backdrop in the distance.

Out there too, a small army of ragged soldiers rode back and forth on their great beasts.

Dragonard guessed the force to number some two

or three hundred. The riders sniped away at Starmarch with a few ray rifles and some blasters whose beams sizzled far short, turning the sand to glass. In the center of the little army was the sonic bombard.

Three men with rags tied around their foreheads rode the tilting, bucking old weapon with the needle-like firing tube. The cannon's airlift mechanism was obviously faulty. The cannon swooped up to heights of four and five feet, then pitched down until no space could be seen between its bottom airports and wind-blasted sand underneath. The gunners held on like horsemen, jerking the lanyard between violent upheavals. At each firing, pale blue vertical rings shot from the needle muzzle. Where the rings touched the wall of Starmarch, the wall caved in.

All over the multi-level battlements, prison guards and Regulators returned fire. Bucking beasts threw riders shot from their seats by the hissing ray-beams. About two dozen of the mounted warriors rode around the army's commander, who carried a tattered piece of bunting on a long pole. The wind unraveled the hunting, showed it scarlet with a human heart-shape of crystal that had glowing golden wire at its center.

"Wave the lantern," Jeremy said. "As soon as they see it, they'll aim the cannon another place to draw attention from us."

Dragonard wigwagged the white light back and forth, back and forth. Out on the plain, the Heart Flag dipped.

Jeremy seized the lantern's turn-key and twisted.

The lantern blacked out. The sonic bombard changed direction, firing at a high turret far to their right.

Jeremy hung on the ramparts, watching the host. Suddenly three riders on beasts broke from the pack and charged the wall. One lifted a tube-muzzled discharger. Dull fire flickered around the barrel's end as the load went off and sent a cord whistling up at them.

The sharpened hooks of a grapnel caught the battlement. Jeremy kicked the prongs in place. He reached over to test the line as one of the riders down below looped the other end around the stamping leg of his beast.

A ray cannon opened up from the tower under bombard attack. Another joined it. The sonic bombard blew up, and vanished in a geyser of thundering sand, screams and blown-off limbs.

"Down the rope," Jeremy said. "Fast, even if it burns the skin off your hands." The tone of command strengthened in his voice with every second.

Dragonard darted for the rope. A blaster beam cut and bubbled the stone of the walkway just in front of him.

He dodged, twisting wildly to keep his footing. Down to the right, three Regulators crouched in the doorway of a watchtower. A blaster bucked in one's hand and part of the battlement a foot from Dragonard puffed away, showering sparks.

"They've got no guns!" one of the Regulators bawled. "Run at them!"

The trio erupted out of the tower, intent on capture. Dragonard lifted the lantern with both hands and flung it like a projectile.

Thc first Regulator caught the sharp metal corner in his temple. He fell back against his mates. The pop of skull-bone reached Dragonard's ears a second later.

Blood leaked down into the Regulator's eyes as he lay on his back, moaning. His companions tried to crawl out from beneath him. Dragonard's mouth hung open and his gold eyes were huge in the glitter of the ray cannons.

He'd killed one of his own. He'd killed a Regulator.

Could the doctors make the lad well? *Pray they could–*

"What's the matter with you?" Jeremy hammered his shoulder. "Down the rope!"

Dragonard climbed the battlement. On the desert the Heart Flag riders wheeled away from the swathe cut by the ray cannons. The riders swept into a crescent and charged away right, raising dust and shrieking and firing their rifles.

The ray cannons swung. Beams cut two, three dozen more from their crude saddles as the head of the column carried the whipping red flag on.

The misdirection worked. Under the deserted wall the three riders motioned for Jeremy and Dragonard to hurry. Dragonard caught the rope, dropped into space and started the long slide down.

His palms screamed and the ground rushed up. He knew there was no going back.

XIII

DRAGONARD STRUCK.

The coarse sand cushioned the impact. He released the line and rolled out of the way. As he scrambled to his feet Jeremy came down swiftly hand over hand. One of the riders indicated the pawing beasts and said to Jeremy, "You take mine, Captain. I'll cut out one with a dead rider."

Captain? Dragonard rubbed his bleeding palms on his trousers. Grains of sand bit the rawness. Jeremy Lynx gave a nod, the quick nod of one accustomed to command respect. His henchman pulled a curved copper knife and slashed the line running up to the battlement. Jeremy grabbed the beast's neck-rope and vaulted up. The smooth, almost effortless mount indicated much experience at desert riding.

Jeremy pointed to Dragonard, said to the man slicing the loops of rope from the beast's foreleg, "Two of you will have to hunt mounts. I want this man to ride with me."

Another man jumped from his saddle. His eyes lit on Dragonard with suspicion but he said nothing.

He flung Dragonard the neck-rope and raced off

after his companion to chase one of the beasts lumbering along without guidance. A dead man dragged in the sand behind the snorting animal, nothing but a seared stump remaining of the rider's head. The man scrambled in close like a monkey and he whacked with his knife, running alongside. The knife blazed in the triple moonglare. The running man cut the neck-rope twisted around the corpse's arm, jumped high, clapped his arms around the beast's neck and went riding after the main Heart Flag host.

"Policemen are notoriously rotten riders," Jeremy said. "If you fall you're on your own. All of these people are my concern. We'll travel fast."

Dragonard wrapped the beast's rope around his left forearm and jumped. He threw a leg over, jerking himself upright onto the saddle which was no more than a kidney-shaped slab of wood, padded and held around the beast's heaving middle by a woven belly-band. Dragonard yanked on the rope. The beast's head swung around and its jaws snapped spitefully. Its diamond-shaped eyes glared and mouth-water drooled over the iron bit.

"I won't fall," Dragonard said. He kicked his knees against the beast's scaled sides and let it feel the bit pulled cruelly hard. The beast turned docile.

" 'Ware the ramparts," said the only man left of the original three rescuers.

Jeremy swung. Regulators were rolling a portable ray cannon toward the place where the grapnel still clung. The main body of the Heart Flag host wheeled away from the walls of Starmarch. Fixed-position ray cannons thundered steadily, thinning out their rear ranks with each blast.

"They have beasts in the fortress pens," Jeremy said. "They'll be after us. I'd love to kill a lot more of them, but prudence says to do otherwise. The horn."

Out went his right hand. Leaning over, the other rider slapped a battered metal trumpet into it. Dragonard thought he detected a grimy, frayed Regulator's regimental tassel hanging from the cord. Jeremy threw his head back and blew into the trumpet.

The metallic sound spread over the desert, thin, faintly off-key. Jeremy slung the trumpet cord around his neck and grinned.

"As a commander, I make do with all sorts of odd equipment. What we lack in prettiness we make up in guts. We're riding for that notch in those crags."

And he yelled blood-curdlingly and kicked his beast into a thunder-footed run.

Dragonard followed and the third rider hammered along beside him. Jeremy yelled for joy, his stubbled face and eyepatch burning in the white light of the moons. Wind cut Dragonard's face.

He had no trouble holding his seat on the lumbering beast, which managed considerable speed and a not altogether uncomfortable ride despite its bulk. The animal flung great exhalations of air, *chu-wuff*, out through the black wet holes of its nostrils. Dragonard found himself smiling, then laughing aloud for the first time in long, tension-wracked hours.

Jeremy sped for a V-notch where the crags angled down to create a pass-like space several riders wide. It was perhaps a mile away across the sandy plain. In from the right poured the steadily rising thunder of the two hundred or so Heart Flag riders still alive. A ray cannon boomed from an oblique angle behind Dragonard. Smoke and a shockwave smote a patch of sand seconds after his beast raced over it.

Already Jeremy's hard riding was a shade too fast for the Starmarch gunners, who had to re-calibrate manually. The portable ray cannon that had been swung up directly behind them went off. This time the charge landed a short distance behind the flying rear feet of Dragonard's beast. Greenish brilliance burst. His shoulders and backbone felt intense heat. The air fumed, chokingly hot suddenly.

Dragonard kicked the beast with his knees. It needed no urging. Its stride lengthened noticeably as it outran the green fireball. *Chu-wuff, chu-wuff,* the gaping nostrils sang the song of its fright.

Then the main body of the host swept around Dragonard, shaking the earth with the passage of the beasts in flight. Tough, hostile faces bobbed to the right and left. Blasters, antique ray rifles, rapiers, crude handmade spears flashed and winked. The Heart Flag soldiers rode with one hand on the rope, or none at all, and carried their weapons ready.

Like a black roaring tide the riders swept out across the sand plain toward the notch. Dragonard was near the head of the charging column. He strove to keep pace with Jeremy but the man rode as though his lower body had melted into the hide of his mount. Both hands free, he waved his companions on, mocking them, daring them to gain more speed.

In the corner of Dragonard's eye came a rippling

motion. He swung, saw the bearer of the Heart Flag pull abreast and survey him. The flag-bearer was a woman.

Her white thighs and arms shone bare in the moon. She wore a man's leather fighting harness that rode up over her hips, its shoulder straps crisscrossed between her high breasts, with only the thinnest of torn and faded tunic cloth between straps and her flesh. Fighter's rings and bronze bracelets jangled on both her arms. Her hair looked a deep red, wine-colored, much darker than the flapping banner whose staff-butt rode in a special socket saddle. She controlled her beast entirely with her legs. In her left hand she carried a shortsword whose blade bore blackish marks, either rust or blood.

Dragonard met her fierce stare with a cold smile as they raced along side by side, both bobbing in the rhythm of the running beasts. The girl's gaze was both curious and hostile. Her face was lovely enough to have graced the Heir Chamber of a Lord of the Exchange. But there was sweat on her forehead, and a piece of rag tied in her foaming red hair to hold it back. She was strange, savage and beautiful as she scrutinized him with eyes that slanted ever so faintly upward from a delicate nose.

Then she cracked a smile with her dry, full lips. Not exactly a defiant smile, as Dragonard's had been . . . a contemptuous one, of dismissal.

"Hiyagggh!"

The guttural cry ripped out of her laughing mouth as she kicked her beast and pulled ahead.

Angered, Dragonard drove his mount to keep up.

Useless. She rode with skill to match Jeremy's, and soon pulled up even with him at the head of the column.

The notch was here. Jeremy plunged into it, then the girl, the flag and her red hair trailing out behind her.

Sound constricted, beat down on Dragonard's ears from the crags on either side. Riders crowded in tight against him. The way was narrow; Dragonard fought for control.

The army never slackened speed as it poured three abreast through the mile-long notch under looming rocks. And in those moments, Dragonard learned a great deal about these unwashed rebels.

If they fought as formidably as they rode, and their dedication matched the intensity of the blood-yells they howled out for no apparent reason, the Heart Flag was indeed a force to be reckoned with.

Black river of mounts and men, the Heart Flag column surged out of the notch and down sandy slopes. A limitless sea-silver plain stretched away, and Dragonard gasped at the sight.

Breathtakingly grand, the North Waste of Pentagon opened ahead, a sweep of emptiness that ran on and on and on. Here and there crags reared, squarish butte-like peaks, towering like monolithic markers of the graves of gods old before II Galaxy knew the tread of Terran men. Onto this immensity where the wind blew strong rode the Heart Flag soldiers.

They strung out into a double file and traveled with no letup. The rider who pounded along beside Dragonard sported the beard, black doublet and gloves of a narcotics runner. The pair of daggers in primitive scabbards at his belt showed him to be a recruit. The man's worn but civilized clothing and the crude daggers complemented one another, creating an image of a mercenary already well adapted to a new, strange land.

They rode for an hour.

Another.

Dragonard's teeth and bones began to ache.

Sand-dust trailed in a cloud behind their passage. The first moon waned and shadows changed direction on the desert floor.

They pounded around the rim of a huge, dry lake that swooped away and down to their left. Thundering on, they left behind a tottered castle ruin on an eminence which, eons ago, must have surveyed a vast span of blue waters. From the single wall still standing, a bird with yellow eyes and wings like great leather blankets shrieked at them, disturbed.

One more hour and Dragonard's whole lower body turned numb. The land of the North Waste began to slope upward. The army charged to the top of a low plateau that ran away to the right and left horizons. Directly ahead on the plateau, displaying many nooks and rough rock faces, one of those gigantic stone monoliths rose. Dragonard guessed it would take a man twenty minutes to ride completely around it. Proud and lost, it reared its craggy splendor at the stars.

Within a short distance of the base of his monument rock, Jeremy raised his arm. The riders slowed down and turned off to right or left and spread out along the lip of the plateau they'd just crested. Dragonard breathed with relief as his beast slowed and stopped.

He climbed down and walked to where Jeremy, already dismounted, stood with the red-haired girl.

Never taking his eyes from the south horizon, Jeremy said, "This is the one, Bel."

The girl's gaze remained unfriendly. "You shouted about him. But in all the clatter of riding hard, I didn't hear."

Struck by her beauty, by the sweet, brutal thrust of her breasts beneath the flimsy undertunic and fighting-harness straps, Dragonard still raged silently because of the contemptuous way she studied him. She held the flagstaff in her right fist. The other fist she planted on her hip. Under the hem of the leather skirt her smooth legs showed satin muscle.

"He helped me escape, Bel." Jeremy said it absently, screwing around and wrenching his head back to stare up the face of the giant rock. "We'll put men up there in the niches and slots. Oh." Jerked back from his thoughts of generalship, he faced the girl and Dragonard again. "We haven't much time for formalities, but his name is—"

"We have no time at all to waste on men who don't belong here," she said. "He's no mercenary. I can tell that from the look of him."

"This is my sister Bel," Jeremy said. "He has his own reasons for wanting to be in the North Wastes—wanting to find the Heart Flag. He's a former policeman. His name's Maxmillion Dragonard."

Crying low, the girl snatched at her sheathed shortsword. "A Regulator?"

Jeremy grabbed her wrist, shoved it down. "Cashiered. His superiors locked him up. You'll hear the whole story when there's time. Right now, sufficient to say I think I trust him. We'll learn for certain whether we can shortly."

Jeremy pulled the trumpet around on its cord and blew another raucous note. No one laughed. Silence dropped.

"We'll stand," Jeremy yelled. He gestured. "Up there, on the rock. Plenty of places. Get into position but first tie up the beasts out behind."

The Heart Flag fighters kicked their mounts. Sand clouds swirled as lines of riders raced around the sides of the rock and vanished into the silver dark beyond.

Dragonard said, "You command a good deal of respect out here."

"I should. I'm in charge of this pitiful bunch of hired thugs and misbegotten idealists."

"And this is your sister?"

"Yes. Bel and I—"

"Dragonard," she breathed. "The one who slew those he caught. I knew I'd heard the name . . . and stories. I've heard the stories in Gannonblock."

"Does that make me acceptable as a recruit?" Dragonard snarled.

"Not completely. You're still a Regulator." Her eyes were green, lovely, tough.

"Save the quarrels."

Jeremy pulled Dragonard's elbow. He moved

with the precise sureness of a man in total command. Dragonard swung, visually following Jeremy's pointing finger. Far across the basin, white pinpoint lights flickered.

"That, Dragonard, is St. Anne, I'll wager. Plus a whole troop of Regulators on beasts. They'll expect us to run. If we do, they'll tire us out and eventually leave us no freedom of movement. I doubt they'll anticipate a stand, which is why I intend to make one." With a humorless grin he clapped Dragonard's shoulder. "And as I said, we'll learn something else in the bargain."

"What's that?" Dragonard already knew.

"Whether you're really on this side. Bel, find him a ray rifle. One with a full charge left in it."

Bel planted the Heart Flag in the sand with a thrust and ran, laughing.

Dragonard's mouth was a slash. "You think a test's still necessary?"

"Very." Grinning, the man pulled off his eyepatch. Two good blue eyes shone. "You're much too close to the heart of the Heart Flag movement if you're not being honest, Dragonard."

He stared at Dragonard as if trying to decipher his thoughts and reaction. Then, talking into the wind's low murmur, he added, "Sometimes, you see, I go by the name Methuselah."

XIV

METHUSELAH, the leader? The faceless name that seemed to mock the dying star kings and had raised the scents of blood and suspicion in old Jonas Valk?

After the stunned surprise Dragonard was exhilarated. Jeremy Lynx, youthful, couldn't be a literal Methuselah; therefore he must be a symbolic one. What did the name mean? Dragonard had no time to speculate now. But if he could stay alive, the riddle might unravel.

Bel returned, to slap the ray rifle into his hands. "I checked the charge chamber: it's ready to go. You'll have no excuse for failing to kill those men coming after us."

His nod was curt. He wouldn't mind finishing St. Anne. But blast down other Regulators? Men like Valk—like himself a while ago—acting out of loyalty, obeying orders? No.

He wondered how much he could remember of ray rifle instruction from the Academy. Could he disarm the mechanism without giving himself away?

Out on the desert the white lights grew. The Heart

Flag fighters broke for the tall rock. They climbed up hand over hand, quiet now. The wind keened.

Bel pulled the banner out of the sand. Its red cloth unfurled and flapped with a ragged defiance. She slung the flag over her shoulder and started away, giving Dragonard one last look.

He cracked a smile. It startled and disarmed her. Her brows pushed together and she quickly corrected the revelation of surprise. Contempt had faded from her eyes completely; suspicion was still there, but with respect, too.

As he headed for the base of the rock, Dragonard thought, *She knows I'm not some criminous little flea hanging on Lynx, at least. She knows I'm a man.* He watched Bel disappear around the rock and appear a moment later on a ledge eight feet up. In the eerie light of the Waste the sides of her strong, smooth legs flashed.

And she's a woman, was his thought then.

He climbed. All over the rock's face, the Heart Flag men dropped into position behind outcrops of rock. From the south a thundering rose. Dragonard found a place on a prow-like point about a quarter of the way up the rock. Bel went halfway to the top; from her post she could look straight down on him.

She passed the flag to her brother. Nimble and quick, Jeremy went to a position just below the summit. There he vanished.

Soon the pursuing force took on definition. It consisted of no more than seventy-five Regulators mounted on beasts. The men wore anti-gas bubble helmets, transparent and shining in the moonglow. Each beast had a collar with a small chemical guide light attached. These, seen as white starspecks from a distance, lit the way ahead of the riders.

The Heart Flag men, expert desert riders, needed no such aid. Dragonard was amused that he was already beginning to think as one of Jeremy's people, to identify with their side.

A quarter mile from the plateau where the monument rock stood, the Regulators reined in. They deployed in a single line for a charge. Behind them a translucent egg-shaped vehicle hovered on its air-lifts. From a communications mast on the egg's top fluttered the pennon of the High Commander. St. Anne was leading the pursuit but taking no chances. The hatch of the command egg did not open. The Regulators evidently were wired to a signal circuit.

Dragonard checked the mechanism plate of the ray rifle. If he could open it . . .

Then he realized he had no tools with which to unfasten the meccano-screws.

He banged his fist on the plate, cursing. He'd have to fire full, killing charges.

From the top of the rock Jeremy's bugle tootled. Oddly, it no longer sounded comic. Ray rifles opened up from all over the rock. Sizzling green bolts hissed down off the plateau but fell short.

The beasts of the Regulators snorted and some hauled back to paw with their front legs. All at once the Regulator line heaved forward. As the ragged charge hurled ahead, the command egg stayed in the same position.

Desperate, Dragonard pressed the stock of the ray rifle against his cheek. He sighted out along the muzzle at a rider's bubble helmet coming up the slope to the plateau top. The Regulators were firing back and green beams going both ways crisscrossed. Rock broke away above him. A huge chunk and a Heart Flag corpse sailed down.

Pull. Pull!

Dragonard couldn't do it. He couldn't gun down one of his own kind. And above him, for certain, Bel would see. . . .

The first Regulators reached the rim of the plateau. A blinding blast of green beams poured off the monument rock. Regulators dropped from their beasts. The seconds ticked out.

Dragonard's face ran with sweat. He had to fire. He *had* to kill—

Just when it seemed most hopeless, a Regulator made it up over the rim and charged the rock. One of the Heart Flag rays touched his anti-gas helmet, splitting it. In the instant before the man's head puffed away, Dragonard saw a swarthy, bearded face, horror-wrenched.

A beard? The regs didn't permit a Regulator to wear—

Laughing loud, Dragonard knew.

Of course St. Anne couldn't continually employ Regulators in reasonably large groups without some of his scheme leaking. Better to juggle the force's credit accounts, of which he had full control, and buy the necessary men. And it would be easier to bribe one or two supply officers to furnish uniforms than to order a whole Regulator troop out like this.

St. Anne was fighting with disguised mercenaries.

Dragonard's finger worked on the trigger. Green light spat from his rifle. A riding man went off his saddle, shrieking. Laughing, Dragonard shot again. Another fell.

The charge broke and turned back, raising dust. The battle lasted only twenty minutes more.

Three times the false Regulators tried a charge up to the plateau. Three times the combination of firepower and concealment gave the advantage to the Heart Flag. Dead beasts with guide lights still burning lay all over the slope and uniformed men littered the sand. The Heart Flag left no wounded. Each corpse was hit twice or three times to insure death.

All at once the fifteen or twenty riders remaining wheeled and converged on the command egg. Within another minute or two, the egg whisked away toward the south horizon with the survivors straggling after it.

Dragonard clambered down the rock along with the others. He checked hurrriedly among the dead, finding enough heads in cracked helmets to assure him that his original judgment had been right: St. Anne hadn't dared to use Regulators for this. Dragonard didn't intend to tell anyone, though.

Already the Heart Flag men were mounting. Casualties had been light, two killed and a handful more wounded. Dragonard found his mount. He saw Bel approaching.

"I watched," she said. "You killed six."

"You didn't watch closely enough. It was seven." He mounted and left her standing.

Climbing onto his own beast nearby, Jeremy overheard. He nodded once and threw a half-smile in Dragonard's direction. That was all the indication of success Dragonard needed. He'd keep his knowledge of the shaving regulations of the galactic police force to himself.

Away like a black froth of river, the Heart Flag rode into the north.

Most of them laughed, some of them sang. Several times Dragonard caught Bel glancing back at him over her shoulder with a new, curious expression on her face.

Interest? That satisfied Dragonard. But Kristin's image never left his mind.

The Heart Flag men rode another two hours and then camped. Meager stocks of old, yeasty food cubes were broken out, together with a swallow of water per man. Jeremy posted pickets. Someone handed Dragonard a scrap of blanket. He rolled into it gratefully, tired and cold.

A babble of voices, a clamor of cursing and joking brought him awake suddenly.

"Well, what the hell," said a voice.

Dragonard came out of the blanket fast. The voice of Tingo Spellhands was unmistakable.

"I thought I recognized a ringer in the sleeping babies," Spellhands said.

Not a foot away, there stood the ex-slaver in the thin bluish light of morning.

Dragonard saw that while he'd slept, the camp had swelled by at least two hundred men and as many beasts. Most of the new arrivals were Pentagon-born warriors, the flat-nosed men with hair to their shoulders and a preference for daggers or spears. But a couple of dozen of the ragtag other-world recruits had come along too, squatting and talking now in small bands.

A peculiar silence rippled out across the camp. Tingo Spellhands flexed his metal hands; the crystal fingers were dark. The ex-slaver wore a filthy tunic and breeches. His right leg ended in a conventional jackboot; his left ended at the knee, the fabric tucked up around the top of a prosthesis which was nothing more than a silver corkscrew of metal whose point dug the ground.

Spellhands' wavy hair danced in the wind. Nearly all of it had turned white. "I detect a certain surprise," he said.

"You're damn right. Where did you come from?"

"Last night? Or earlier? You know where I was you saw me last." The slap, the insult, with a wrench of the lips to add malice: "Commander."

"Last night will do. Are you taking Heart Flag money?"

"Um." Spellhands nodded. "I came in with the band that's been patrolling and waiting to link up with our leader soon as he was broken loose."

"You hired on, then."

"But of course, Commander." Spellhands indicated the corkscrew prosthesis, an unflexing spring-shape with a sharp tip. "Minus a leg, which I owe to you, I had to find some way to pay for this cheapjack job of fixing me up. I went over the

Rankor wall, blood and stump and all. Your outfit didn't pay the slightest attention. Never mind how I made it to Pentagon, or who sold me the metal leg, or how I heard about the Heart Flag. I've got contacts in the less scrupulous trades, you know. But what really matters now that I run into you here is not even why *you're* here—just *that* you're here." Spellhands made a tentative motion with one hand toward the other, toward the hand with the switch. "I never dreamed I'd see you. I imagine there was quite a party, too. Wine and songs in the skysled when you all celebrated how you'd tipped the prison break and got me this."

The soft *clang* as Spellhands bent and hit the corkscrew murmured in the stillness.

"I didn't know the Regulators were coming."

Spellhands said a filthy word. The hate in him could almost be physically felt. Dragonard's gold eyes were alert. He was fully awake, watching for an attack. He was conscious of someone running to the far side of the camp, summoning Jeremy, summoning Bel.

It took iron restraint for Dragonard to keep from attacking first. It took every bit of it he had to remember the mission, to try to sound tractable, convincing.

"The Regulators surprised me as much as they did you. They wanted me for an assignment. They promised me freedom if I went along. I took them up on it but it didn't work out. I had to break away from them. We're both still criminals, my friend, just the way we were on Rankor."

There was a flurry of men stepping aside as Jeremy appeared, cold-eyed and bundled in a coarse red cloak. His snarl interrupted another curse from Spellhands.

"What's this all about? We're supposed to be moving out."

"A little reunion, sir," Spellhands replied. He showed Jeremy deference. "Your police friend is the reason I'm walking around less than a whole man." Spellhands couldn't maintain the deferential tone. In tangled, chopped sentences, he spat out the essence of what had happened during the prison break. "That's a debt I owe the Commander and one I'll pay."

"All right," Dragonard said. "We'll get it over with right now."

"Damn if you will," Jeremy said softly.

"I'm going to kill him sometime," said Dragonard. "It might as well be now."

"Dragonard helped me break out of the Regulator prison," Jeremy said to Spellhands. "So keep your peace or you'll be out of these ranks. I'll turn you loose with no water and no beast. I'm paying you to help us keep the Regulators away and that's *all* the fighting I'm paying for."

Spellhands' cheek developed a tic, a violent one. "But he's a God damn policeman himself!"

"I tried to explain it, Jeremy," Dragonard said. "He won't believe I'm running from St. Anne too."

Jeremy stared at Spellhands. "You'd better."

Dragonard's anger couldn't be bridled. "I want to get it over."

Spellhands clicked the crystal tips of his fingers faintly, one hand against another. "I do too. God love me, how I do, you strutting, high-assed f—"

Up washed the redness, a blinding burst of it behind Dragonard's eyes. He lunged.

Jeremy was faster. Stepping into the path, he swung and brought a hard fist up against Dragonard's belly. Dragonard took the blow with an outpouring of breath. He rocked on his feet but didn't fall. Jeremy walked up and down between them, furious.

"No fighting. How clear must I make it? No fighting or I'll abandon both of you." He turned to Spellhands. "And you remember who I am. Remember that when I vouch for the policeman, that ends it. Whether you think it ends it or not, that ends it."

"I'm going to kill him," Spellhands said.

Whiteness drove the color from Jeremy's cheeks. He backhanded Spellhands' face twice.

Then he got control of himself. A silent ring of fighting men watched as Jeremy said, "Not in my camp."

Somehow Spellhands gained control. He actually managed a smile. "Then later."

"Just remember the warning," Jeremy said. "I'll put you adrift in the Waste and you'll never find your way out."

With a glare at Dragonard as if to say the threat applied to him as well, Jeremy made an abrupt turn. He clapped his hands.

"Get the beasts! I don't want to ride in daylight

any longer than necessary. They can spot us from skysleds flying out of firing range.'' He gave the man nearest him a hard shove on the shoulder. Instantly the crowd broke.

Only Spellhands remained, and Dragonard. They stared at each other.

The Heart Flag men ran for the tether-stakes and began ripping the rope knots loose. The beasts snorted and blew through their black nostrils and lifted themselves up from dozing position on their huge scaled legs. Still Dragonard and Spellhands watched one another.

Tingo Spellhands turned his corkscrew prosthesis a quarter turn in the sand. Then he chuckled and shrugged simultaneously, as if dismissing Dragonard. But the hate lingered in his eyes as he walked away.

Slowly Dragonard wiped his palms on his legs. It would have been better to finish it. Now he had the threat of the ex-slaver to hamper him.

A beast cut toward him from the right. Bel's red hair danced out behind her in the brightening sunlight as she reined in and leaned down.

``I still have almost as many suspicions of you as Tingo does, policeman.''

He wondered at the use of the first name. ``That's something we'll have to change.''

``Last night I would have doubted you could. Now I'm not so certain.''

With a provocative laugh, almost daring him, she kicked the beast and hammered off.

A damn attractive female . . . strong, beautiful.

Kristin's face intruded. He put them both out of his mind and went to find his saddle and his animal.

The Heart Flag rode north again, pushing for speed. Even with the huge blue sun standing high at midday the Waste was cool, indicating they were moving deeper into the north. Jeremy allowed a ten minute halt for food, then the ride continued. The sand was limitless, blurring at the horizon. After another hour a black smear northward indicated a whole rampart of rock peaks rising to meet them.

Toward midafternoon Spellhands rode up beside Dragonard and shouted in the galloping din: "Jeremy's red-headed sister—she's a special friend, policeman."

"She didn't tell me that."

"No? I saw you talking to her. Don't."

"I'll talk to her when I want, slaver."

Spellhands' whitened hair whipped in the drive of wind. "Yes, I figured you'd say it that way. Well"—his fingers writhed, crystal and metal, around the tether rope—"that'll be one more thing to settle for, Commander. They say these riding animals have long memories. I only want to assure you mine's a hell of a lot longer. And stronger."

Wheeling, he rode back toward the rear of the column. Dragonard could hear him singing.

XV

AT NIGHTFALL Jeremy sent scouts racing ahead. The peaks glimpsed earlier took on clarity, etched in the white of the first moon's rising. Dragonard judged the range to be about ten to twenty miles wide, and perhaps the same distance away from where the Heart Flag host rode now.

The army jogged at a more leisurely pace after the coming of darkness. The desert became less flat, rolling out in front of them in softly domed peaks and low troughs which cut off sight lines and made forward scouts necessary.

All day Bel had ridden beside her brother. But shortly after the darkness settled she cantered back along the column. Was she really Spellhands' woman? Dragonard wondered. Or had he established his priority only in his own mind?

The questions went unanswered. Dragonard saw an opportunity.

He dug his knees in, pulled on the bit to break the beast out of the jogging double file of riders and bolted ahead. Out in front of a brace of scurvy-looking former armor smugglers from Iamb's

Planet, one of whom carried the Heart Flag now, Jeremy rode alone.

Dragonard galloped up and swung in alongside the young commander.

Jeremy was watching the undulating sand hills ahead, as though searching for something. He acknowledged Dragonard's arrival.

"I thought you'd be along to talk before much more time passed." He swung round, his blue eyes unmistakably stern. "A talk's a good idea. But I don't want to hear anything about your feud with our friend with the mechanical fingers. Keep it to yourselves."

A tight nod from Dragonard acknowledged. "I only want to ask one question about him. Why'd you hire him?"

"I didn't. My recruiters in Gannonblock did. I accepted him because he looked like a killer and I need killers to fight this war. If it's any consolation, I tend to take your side in the dispute. In private only, of course. I gather he has a certain brutal charm for women. Bel rather took to him. Until she saw you," he added after a pause.

Jeremy's smile was thin. He went on, "She's the one I feel sorriest for. It's no life out here in this damn wilderness with the whole of II Galaxy against us. Or at least one of the biggest power blocks—the Regulators. I don't suppose the poor clods living on the generosity of the Lords of the Exchange on the planets know about us."

"I suspect they don't. But I don't know very much either."

"And you want some answers to questions. Well, maybe and maybe not."

"What do you mean?"

"A lot of your questions will be answered when we get where we're going. If we get there." His blue eyes moved across the dunes, searching the still night.

"Why are you and your sister doing this?" Dragonard asked.

"Running this snip of an army? We believe what we're doing is right. The Heart Flag stands for something."

"For what, Jeremy?"

The claw-pads of the beasts drummed softly, rhythmically.

"In good time, Max."

It was maddening, the man's cryptic refusal to talk. Dragonard said, "All right. A new tack. What's the meaning of that banner? The crystal heart with wire inside?"

"The Heart Flag stands for everything the Lords of the Exchange have repressed. And that is a lot more than just all the people of II Galaxy."

"Repressed? What have they repressed?"

Again Jeremy pointed to the horizon, the rock ramparts.

"Better you see it first, Max. Then it'll carry more weight than my telling it."

"You're rebelling against the star kings for reasons to be explained."

"Yes."

"The star kings are dying, Jeremy."

Wolfish, he laughed. "Yes. It's the only good thing that's happened since we organized."

Dragonard persisted. "Is there a cause-and-effect relationship?"

"If there isn't, I'm turning my sister into a blood-lusting spinster for nothing." A certain cruel humor, perhaps self-torture, tinctured his words and expression. It was quickly gone.

"How do you pay these people who fight for you?"

"Not all of them are paid, obviously. A lot of them are Pentagon men from the desert villages in the northwest. I recruited there for nearly six months. They're tough, very loyal, and not at all stupid for near-primitives. When I told them the truth and threw in a few promises of some booty which at this stage is simply wishful thinking, they followed me. To get the professionals I sent a few recruiters out on ships to spread the word on the nearby planets. There hasn't been a good minor war in a generation. There were plenty of men on the run and eager for some credits to be earned riding and killing. As to where the money comes from, it's mostly in a blind account in a Federated Creditbanc on Alpha Mu. My father earned handsome sums while he—but never mind that yet. Getting the raw credits in to pay my men is another problem entirely. I'm four months in arrears right now. We have logistics problems, as you might guess. My only salvation is the public tally I make once a week. I show how much I owe each man. They go along because there's no place to spend the wages out here." Jeremy fixed him with a quick glance. "By the way, we've never gone into detail about why you're here. I'd like to hear it from the beginning—from the prison break. I gather that's where Spellhands lost his leg."

So Dragonard told him of Valk, of Valk's plan, and how the High Commander of the Regulators had branded loyalty as treason. Then: "The High Commander doesn't want anyone to know what you're up to. I wonder if he knows himself."

Jeremy nodded. "Oh, he knows. The Lords know too."

"But I have to wait until we get to those mountains."

"I told you. I want understanding, not just comprehension. I—"

Suddenly a beast and rider lunged up to the crest of the dune ahead. The rider reined in. He fisted his right hand, shot it up and down several times in a pumping motion.

Jeremy stiffened. "Hold up!" he shouted over his shoulders.

The long column came to a halt. Wind crooned and lifted whorls of silvered sand; the second moon was rising. Jeremy faced Dragonard again.

"I told you it wouldn't be easy to get where we're going. I want you to see that for yourself. Come on."

He kicked his mount. Dragonard followed. At the top of the rise Jeremy conferred with the scout and the rider drummed on back to the column. Then Dragonard and Jeremy rode down into the trough between this dune and the next.

There Jeremy dismounted and tied his tether-rope

and Dragonard's together. One of the beasts bent its forelegs and dropped down to doze. Jeremy started up the next slope.

"On your belly at the top," he said.

They crawled the last five yards using knees and elbows. At the summit Dragonard raised his head and sucked in a long, startled breath.

From here northward the Waste leveled out again, running away toward the peaks. Not far from the base of this dune, a metal cylinder six feet in diameter and twice that in height rose out of the sand. The fastenings of its armorplate glistened like a thousand blind eyes.

About one hundred yards to the left stood another emplacement; a third rose a similar distance to the right. Like fencing-posts the cylinders marched away in a curving line, one end running toward the northeast horizon, another toward the northwest.

Dragonard realized he was staring at the rim of a mammoth circle of emplacements . . . a circle perhaps twenty to thirty miles in diameter, a circle which encompassed the low peaks ahead.

"Electrogun pillboxes," Dragonard murmured. "Men in them?"

"No, these are automated. We've tried to get at the cable complexes, but they're buried more than forty feet down. We haven't the tools."

A wand-like muzzle pointed out from each emplacement. All of the wands projecting from all of the pillboxes pointed in the direction Dragonard was looking.

North.

It made no sense! At least not instantly. Then part of the backward reason for it hit him, while Jeremy talked low.

"The pillboxes are equipped with temperature sensors which detect our body temperatures unless we're very careful. And—what the hell's wrong with you, Max?"

"The electroguns are pointing inward."

"Congratulations. It's a huge, circular defense line. A complete three hundred and sixty degrees, ringing those mountains. It was installed secretly last winter. The cost must have been fantastic."

"The guns are guarding something," Dragonard went on, thinking out loud. "A ring of electroguns guarding the mountains and they're pointing inward. The guns aren't to keep people out, are they? Their purpose is to keep people in."

Blown sand ticked against Dragonard's cheek as Jeremy said, "To keep people and something else in. We sneak in and out. It's devilish risky but there's no other way. We have to get through those lines now to get where we're going. What the electroguns keep inside that ring is what the Heart Flag is all about." A pause. "Well, shall we see whether we can outwit the sensors one more time?"

XVI

THE TWO MEN crawled back down the dune. At the bottom Jeremy stood up and brushed sand from his garments.

Ahead, the black clot of the Heart Flag host waited. Some of the men had dismounted and another water ration was passing. Near the forefront of the little army Dragonard saw Bel. Her beast kneeled to rest but she remained in the saddle, one hand shielding her eyes against the glare of the third moon rising behind the peaks. The way she leaned slightly forward indicated tension. A quietness among the fighting men told Dragonard that most of them, too, knew about the electrogun barrier.

As they walked along Dragonard said, "The Heart Flag operates from those mountains?"

"Correct."

"Jonas Valk had the impression you had no headquarters, that you ranged all over the Waste."

"We've tried to convey that impression. Unfortunately St. Anne and his crowd know very well where we are and what we're doing. They're besieging us inside that ring, you see."

Dragonard's gold eyes showed puzzlement. "A siege is pretty damn old-fashioned."

"But also, my friend, it's very quiet. We have no skysleds, no way to come out or go in except on beast-back. I should imagine the Regulators whom St. Anne's commanding will find it easier to keep their activities secret if they ride too. Isn't it true that all skysleds have flight recorders?"

A nod from Dragonard. "I see what you mean. For a treasonous operation, it would be better to stay out of the air and leave no record of where you're going."

Jeremy faced Dragonard, the intensity of his expression adding years to him.

"We have very little with which to fight them, Max. Nothing but a secret, really. Provided we can keep control of that secret—provided we can hang on long enough—we can do what we set out to do."

"And what's that?"

Jeremy said, "Bring the Lords of the Exchange to their knees."

The hackles on Dragonard's neck itched. "Overthrow them? You're mad."

"Not at all. The secret buried in those peaks—the secret St. Anne is trying so hard to keep bottled up—is pure power. The power to—"

Abruptly Jeremy grinned. It was the merry, reckless grin Dragonard remembered from Fortress Starmarch. Yet he sensed the shallowness of the smile as Jeremy hit him lightly on the shoulder.

"You'll see it all soon. We want the star kings to capitulate. You probably think that's immoral."

"Would you blame me? I was raised to revere them."

"That's why my words won't convince you. Nothing will convince you, I think, deep in what passes for a heart in a man like you, except seeing the secret firsthand. Seeing it, you'll understand the blasphemy the Lords have committed all these centuries in the name of benevolent rule. You'll know that I designed that flag"—he pointed to the banner which one of the silent, waiting men carried in a saddle-socket—"to throw the truth in their faces like a piece of manure. To make them smell the truth of somebody else knowing what they've done."

A slight tremor shook Jeremy's shoulders. Dragonard wanted to ask another question but he refrained until the ugliness of emotion passed from the young leader's face.

They resumed walking toward the waiting army. After a few strides Dragonard asked, "Can you tell me why you were in Starmarch?"

"Of course. I wasn't caught recruiting, which might be your original guess. Some of us have to leave the siege area now and then for food supplies. Traders in Gannonblock—the few with a liking for high risks and high profit—will take a chance and fly in what we need in a skysled. I pay them well for the risks they take."

"Quite a risk," Dragonard agreed. "I suppose like every planet, Pentagon has its air traffic monitoring system. The skies are watched—"

"Scrupulously. And the traders take bigger risks on a world like this, where skysleds are few and traffic outside the cities almost non-existent. One of the traders approached the Regulators for a bigger payment than the one I'd promised. I walked into a trap. Fortunately I'd never dealt with the trader as Methuselah. I'd posed as an outsider acting as agent for the Heart Flag. That's why I wound up simply imprisoned and not depth probed."

They had reached the edge of the host. Bel handed Jeremy his trumpet when he motioned and Jeremy blew three short, ragged notes.

From the main body of the small army a dozen men ran forward to group around their leader. From her saddle Bel studied Dragonard, half-smiling. He met her glance, defied it, turned his attention to Jeremy.

As he swept his gaze around to the leader, Dragonard saw Tingo Spellhands watching him from several ranks back, leaning against the shoulder of his kneeling beast. He ran a metal finger back and forth over his upper teeth. Half his face was shadow-black, half sprayed with moonlight. One eye burned, watchful.

Jeremy spoke: "Kardrak, you and Miles will be in charge of the fireballs."

"We're already rolling up the blankets and lashing them together," answered one of the lieutenants.

"Good. How is our supply of armament oil?"

"Low. We'll use all we have to get the balls burning."

"That's all right, we have more in the mountains. Start the balls between the fifth and sixth electroguns down the line to the left. I'll give you ten minutes to get in position. When I give two blasts on the horn, that's your signal."

The pair of men gave ragged salutes and raced back among the rest. To the others Jeremy said, "Each of you is responsible for keeping your groups together. Some of these off-worlders don't know much about Regulator technology, so remind them. No one gets within three feet of an emplacement. Go that close and the sensors will pick up the change in temperature even with the fireballs burning. Three feet is the absolute limit. I expect you to shoot or stab any man or beast that even comes close to putting the rest of us in danger. Clear?"

A growled murmur of understanding. Jeremy waved them away.

During the next ten minutes the Heart Flag army broke into smaller bands of twenty to thirty riders each which then rode slowly forward to the crest of the long dune overlooking the ring of cylinders. Dragonard followed Jeremy and Bel. He noted that each band positioned itself on the dune-top so that it could ride straight forward and through the line at a point equidistant from the emplacements on its right and left.

The wind sang and the peaks ahead glimmered and shone, tantalizing.

The secret. Dragonard kept thinking those words. *The secret.*

What was it? What could it be to produce the almost unthinkable overthrow of the Lords?

He was inclined to scoff. Everything in his upbringing made the Lords sacred, all-powerful, almost holy figures beyond reach and reproach. Only when he gazed at Jeremy's hawk profile and saw the intensity of the young man's determination did Dragonard manage to check his judgment. Check it, at least, until they passed the perilous electrogun lines and reached the mountains.

Up and down the line of the dune, riders shifted nervously. Jeremy raised his old bugle and blew the two notes. They died away eerily in the night air.

Away to the left, fire burst. A long, startled "*Ahhhh!*" ripped from the mouths of the riders. Three good-size, rope-wrapped balls of blankets had been set on fire. From a position about ten feet in front of one of the emplacements, men hurled the fireballs north.

Trailing sparks, the fireballs dropped just inside the electrogun perimeter and blazed.

A machine-like whirring came from the cylinders, filling the night. The sensors had caught the instant increase in temperature. The cylinders on either side of the fire rotated with a ponderous squeal of metal. It took just a few seconds for every wand-like muzzle up and down the line for a mile to swing and point at the leaping flames.

Then crackling blue lines of light shot from the wands, converging on the fireballs.

Jeremy slashed his raised hand downward. The Heart Flag host rode.

Plunging down the slope, Dragonard hauled on the bit. His beast tended to angle to the left. Dragonard brought him back in line, sighting to the mid-point between the two emplacements directly ahead.

Sizzle-and-crack, the electroguns discharged at intervals of three or four seconds. Because the wands projected from the very tops of the cylinders, angling their fire downward toward the fireballs already beginning to gutter out, the riders would have no difficulty passing beneath the lethal beams.

They crossed the line. Cylinders flashed past him on right and left.

Jeremy led the charge, riding hard. Dragonard felt intense heat on the top of his head as he thundered beneath the discharging wand. Then cooler wind fanned his face.

Jeremy rode on for another couple of hundred yards where he and Bel reined in. Dragonard came up beside them. The other groups of Heart Flag riders, not quite so swift, were just now passing between various cylinders.

Up on the desert to the left the fireballs disappeared as all the converging electrogun beams created a whirling blue firestorm that consumed the air around it. The night echoed with the thunder of the beasts and the sizzling of the wands firing, firing, firing.

Two more groups of riders passed safely through. Only two remained, one to the right of where Dragonard sat his beast, another to the left. The front riders of both groups crossed the line, kicking their mounts hard.

The first group got through safely. The second,

the one on the left, showed some confusion in its ranks. Beasts bucked and butted against one another and men yelled. The group's swift, orderly progress dissolved in a chaos of cries and animal snorts.

Jeremy strained forward in his saddle to see. "What the hell's wrong there?"

The fireballs had disappeared. Night closed down again. The electrogun emplacements began to rotate back to their original positions. Two of the riders in the beleaguered group fell out of their saddles. Dragonard saw one falling man's silhouette clearly against the stars.

A shortsword stuck from his backbone.

The man hit the sand, dead or dying. Dragonard's throat tightened to yell a warning, but Jeremy saw too. He slapped his beast's neck and drove it into a run.

Bel rode right behind him. Several others, including Dragonard, followed. The pattern was becoming clear. A single rider in the struggling group was lashing around him with a dagger and hauling on his reins to break free of the other riders who swarmed around him, aware of sudden treachery.

Out of the brawling pack a cry drifted: "The slaver killed McDue! He's going for the cylinders. *Stop him, somebody!*"

Swords hacked and flashed. The rider with the dagger drove his blade into the belly of a man trying to club him with a spear butt and the dead man reeled back in his saddle. Reinless, his beast pawed and snorted. The terrified animal crashed against several others, opening a path out of the press.

The renegade rider wheeled and broke into a charge toward the nearest cylinder. In the moonglare hands of metal and crystal flashed, gripping reins.

"Spellhands!" Dragonard yelled.

Jeremy wigwagged his arms ferociously, trying to catch Spellhands' attention. The ex-slaver was riding fast on a course which would take him well within three feet of an emplacement.

"Turn off!" Jeremy bawled. "Man, turn off or you'll trigger the sensors—"

"He knows what he's doing," Dragonard howled into the wind.

Spellhands crashed his beast against the cylinder, bucked back away from it, turned and rode wildly straight at Jeremy, Bel and Dragonard.

Hate-bloated, his face caught the moon. He was laughing.

Pandemonium struck. The heat of Spellhands' body and that of his animal triggered the cylinder and started it rotating. Up and down the line other interlinked cylinders hummed again, turning. The nearest electrogun spat and crackled.

Jeremy literally jumped from his saddle. He hurled himself through the air to the right to knock Bel from her mount. They tumbled to the sand. The sizzle-and-crack struck Bel's beast.

The animal screamed. Its whole body glared with a luminous blue halation. In a puff of smoke the beast melted into wiggling, glutinous jelly that spread across the sand.

Dragonard hauled on his bit, not quite knowing which way to turn. Other electroguns opened up.

The nearer ones aimed at the group of men in which Spellhands had been riding. Seeing the trouble, riders already safely out on the desert turned back. Jeremy yelled at them to stay away but the noise drowned him out. Electroguns down the line swiveled to aim at the Heart Flag men riding in to aid their companions.

Blue-sizzling light glared near Dragonard's head. He drove his beast to the left, barely getting out of the way in time. The electrogun bolt decimated half the riders still floundering to reorganize themselves after Spellhands' attack.

Spellhands himself pounded right toward Bel and Jeremy, who floundered ankle-deep in the sand. Men screamed. Blinding blasts of blue tore the night as more and more of the electroguns started firing from up and down the perimeter.

Spellhands' face lighted with the blue wash as he reined up over Jeremy and Bel. His cheeks ran with sweat. He pulled and pulled on the reins until his beast's forelegs lifted. He intended to smash down on Jeremy's head.

Lithe and quick, Jeremy darted out of the way. Bel hurled against Spellhands' flank, tearing at his leg with her bare hands. Spellhands hooked an elbow around her neck. He levered viciously. Dragonard drove his mount toward them.

The sizzle-and-crack of the electrogun wands blotted out all sounds except the strident cries of the Heart Flag men who were being roasted to death by twos and threes and tens. The cylinders were sensing entire groups of the riders now. The electroguns fired separately at the humans nearest them.

Blue light—burned skin—smell—screaming.

The infiltration had become a destruction.

"Teach you," Spellhands was blithering as he simultaneously tried to jockey his mount around to crack Jeremy's head and hung on to Bel's thrashing body with his elbow. *"Teach you to tell Tingo Spellhands who he can kill and who he can't!"*

Down came his mount's forelegs. Jeremy scrambled aside just in time. The beast's pads thudded sand.

Dragonard plunged in, dodging a blue beam. Weaponless, he halved the distance between himself and the revenge-crazed slayer. He leaped his animal across a pond of smoldering red and gray stuff that had been half a dozen Heart Flaggers a moment ago.

Spellhands saw him coming. He looked insanely gleeful. Spellhands relaxed his elbow, dropped his hand and caught the belt of Bel's leather fighting harness. With one jerk he pulled her up and across his saddle and his spread thighs. Then he swung his mount around and gave it its head.

The terrorized beast loped straight north, out of the range of the electroguns.

Bel struggled, hanging head-down across Spellhands' mount. Her dark red hair streamed out along the heaving animal's scaled side.

On his feet, Jeremy couldn't walk properly. His right leg had gotten twisted somehow so that it buckled under him. Horror lay on his face as he assessed the destruction of the electroguns.

Nearly half the Heart Flag host had disappeared in those awful, stinking welters of heaving jelly. Seeing that the only safety lay in quick retreat, the rest of the riders were thundering north in ragged formation, some minus an arm or a leg. One man rode by with nothing left at his right shoulder but a smoky gray stump that shone wet as fresh glue.

"I can't walk," Jeremy screamed at Dragonard. "You get after her—"

The wind carried the words away. Dragonard jerked his beast's head, turning it toward the mountains. Northward, he could dimly make out Spellhands riding hard with Bel still flung kicking across his saddle.

Dragonard's gold eyes lit with hate, and he rode.

XVII

PURSUED AND PURSUER, they thundered under the triple moons for a good five minutes.

Slowly, slowly, Dragonard's huge beast drew closer. The gaping black nostrils went *chu-wuff, chu-wuff* in steady rhythm. Spellhands glanced back over his shoulder often. His face looked wet, uncertain. His white hair flew.

Dragonard pushed the beast without mercy. A swift look to the rear showed him that the electroguns no longer flared. Those who remained of the Heart Flag soldiers had disappeared in the shifting silver-and-dark uncertainty of the desert. Dragonard faced front again, his skin pushed into ugly planes by the force of the wind.

Again Spellhands glanced back. Undirected, his beast plunged across the top of a low dune and hurtled down the other side. Spellhands swayed in the saddle, off balance. He jerked at the reins. The beast rebelled at the bit's bite and faltered. Spellhands pitched from the saddle.

Bel slid down after him. The beast raised its scaled

head, snorted and broke into a bounding run, away to freedom.

A brutal chuckle rose like bubbles in Dragonard's throat. Spellhands floundered in the sand at the top of the dune. Dragonard reached its base in less than a minute. He reined in and jumped down.

Spellhands stood at the dune's top, the smaller of the three moons a burning white backdrop for his bobbing head.

"Come on," he shouted down. "Come on, Commander."

Dragonard took the invitation and walked up the duneside in ankle-deep sand. A rock skittered against his boot. He bent without breaking stride and picked it up. Fear ran through him like heat. Counterbalancing it, the redness seeped and ebbed at the edges of his mind.

Somewhere to the right, Bel moaned incoherently. She was stunned by her fall. Spellhands tried to light his hands. The left one flickered intermittently. As Dragonard brought his forearm up to shield his eyes the flickering stopped.

Spellhands spewed out one obscene curse after another. The power cell had run out. Dragonard lowered his arm. He was nearly halfway up the dune. Spellhands fumbled at his belt. Laughing, he slashed the empty air twice.

Spellhands still had his dagger. He flourished it once more.

Moonlight flamed off Spellhands' corkscrew prosthesis; slobber rolled down his chin.

"I'm waiting, Policeman. I'm waiting to settle up."

In all his years as a Regulator, Dragonard had learned a lesson: life was too desperately precious to be thrown away with a chivalric gesture. Without breaking stride he flung the rock to gain the advantage, and followed it in a charge that took Spellhands by surprise.

The rock chucked off Spellhands' forehead. Arms wide, Dragonard leaped. He hit Spellhands below the waist and closed his arms hard and pitched him backward.

Screaming, Spellhands tumbled down the other side of the dune. He cut the air with the dagger, hitting nothing.

Up instantly, Dragonard spotted the rock. He snatched it up and raced down the slope. Spellhands recovered, gaining his footing, grabbed a handful of sand and threw it hard, like a man sowing seed against the wind.

Some of the prickly grains struck Dragonard's eyes. He rubbed them and kept moving. Spellhands lunged.

Dragonard darted aside. He chopped for the back of Spellhands' neck with the rock but Spellhands had the speed of the crazed and Dragonard missed.

Around came Spellhands, crouching, drool leaking from both corners of his mouth. He kept smiling. Spellhands feinted with the blade; Dragonard executed a back-step.

Spellhands giggled, a wet sound.

"Frightened of me, Policeman? Yellow, Policeman?"

Redness rose and rose inside Dragonard. The quaking began to work its way along his limbs. He feinted to the left with the rock. Spellhands responded, lifting his dagger high. Dragonard knew he was losing control. The red light played inside his mind, searchlight-bright.

He feinted again; Spellhands didn't respond. Shifting to the right, Dragonard threw the rock.

With a stumbling step, Spellhands got out of the way. Dragonard caught two handfuls of sand and threw them. Spellhands squealed and batted at his eyes. Dragonard ran in under his guard and punched with his right fist.

He put all his strength into his hand, burying it in Spellhands' middle. He drove his left up under Spellhands' breastbone.

Spellhands doubled and started to pull back out of the way. Dragonard's right boot slipped from under him in the uncertain sand.

Spellhands had a brief target—Dragonard's exposed spine. He smashed his right hand of metal and crystal over and down, blindingly fast.

Dragonard screamed as the dagger went to the hilt in his back.

Pain and seething red pushed at the boundaries of his mind. Sand, sand. Grainy. Insubstantial. Slipping between his fingers—

He crawled away on hands and knees. Spellhands whooped and cackled and practically danced with joy.

In his fingers Dragonard felt the rock, smooth, cold, oval. He came up and around with his teeth bared like an animal's. The wound bled soggy warmth down his back. The knife stuck from his spine like a black cross. He ran.

Spellhands whirled, not expecting the attack, and Dragonard cracked the rock against his mouth, breaking half his front teeth.

Spellhands went down and Dragonard crawled on top of him, seeing the man's face only partially.

Crystal fingers ripped at Dragonard's cheeks and throat. He hardly felt it. A scarlet image of Spellhands' face occupied the whole visible universe, bigger than all of creation. Dragonard used the bloody, slippery rock. He hit with it, hit, hit, hit, hit.

Spellhands' nose disappeared; his eyesockets ran with gore. Dragonard crashed the rock down and crashed it and crashed it. Spellhands' frontal skull bones fragmented; bits of bone thrust through skin; grayish stuff weltered up.

Dragonard no longer even resembled a man. He worried Spellhands' body with the rock, bone by bone, hitting until bone's solidity turned to pulp. The redness controlled him and he let it. A wild image of electrical circuits smoking, sparking, burning out slid in and out of his mind.

Dead, something told him after many minutes. *Dead.*

Panting and covered with a slime of blood, Dragonard crawled to his feet. One boot squashed down into the mess that had been Tingo Spellhands. He reached around to pull at the dagger in his back but he couldn't reach it. He knew he was mortally wounded.

The redness receded a little and Bel's face appeared against the burning cyclorama of the moon-hung sky.

Dragonard said obscene things about the dead

man. Bel's arms went around him. His bloody lips tasted salt tears on her face. She kissed him full-mouthed and cried but to him it felt like kissing cold stone. All his fingers were frozen. The chill was stealing up from his ankles into his trunk, sending out shoots of frost through his belly toward his heart.

Weeping, Bel said his name. Dragonard saw the triple moons slide together into an eruption of whiteness.

Ah, God, I don't want to die, he thought, and went down into cold, bottomless murk.

Layers of darkness prevented him from seeing them but he knew, somehow, that they were there. Were the voices ghosts?

No, not quite yet, he reasoned. But soon, now. Soon.

Jeremy saying: "Can you hear, Max? Can you hear anything?"

And Bel: "He stirred a little."

"—palliative drugs." That was Jeremy again. "—the best we have and all we carry in our field kits. I've gotten the stragglers together. There are about forty men left. We'll try to get you home. We might have a chance that way. The ride will be hard on you. It's not far. The drugs may help a little—"

"He's going to die," Bel said, far off.

Exhausted, Dragonard searched for light at the far end of the tunnel of his mind, saw none.

"—we carry one small diagnostic machine. There's an indication that your brain's been fatally and fundamentally damaged. *Dragonard?*"

"He doesn't hear you," Bel's voice echoed.

I could have told you that, Dragonard said in the awesome silence of pain and dark. *I went farther with Spellhands than I ever went before. It was a brighter red than I ever saw. An image of wires buring out. Smoking. Smelling. All the brain circuits overloading–ah, I could have told you–*

"Give him another injection." Jeremy's voice faded. "Then let's mount and move out."

The weeping of Bel blended with a soft thunder of shuffling beasts, a murmur of men.

Oddly, Dragonard felt tranquil. Perhaps it was because he knew struggling was useless.

His last thought was, *This is a hell of a way for a policeman to die.*

XVIII

A HAND HELD an old silver-backed mirror in front of his face.

In the mirror he saw a face which resembled his own. The hair of his head had been shaved away at some time and now it had begun to grow back, sparse white-streaked stubble. But he was unable to see the most startling, unusual feature of the face which regarded him with gold eyes.

Beginning just below each ear, a stitchless red seam of scar tissue rose vertically to each temple. From there the two scar lines converged upward and inward, meeting at a point near the top center of his head. The scar immediately suggested a whole flap of skin being peeled away—scalp, forehead, upper cheeks—and replaced. Indeed, the flesh over the cheekbones had a new, drum-like tautness across the bone.

"You have what amounts to a new brain," said Jeremy. His hand held the mirror.

Maxmillion Dragonard watched the mirror face, still stunned. Jeremy smiled. He was obviously enjoying Dragonard's surprise.

Dragonard lay on a low bed of tikwood pegged together, a fur blanket covering him. He wore pantaloons and a long-sleeved tunic of cheap woven cloth.

The small chamber flickered and shifted in the light thrown by an oil lamp sitting in a wall niche. A low slot window in one of the stone walls offered a view of jutting battlements and turrets much resembling Fortress Starmarch. Panicstricken, Dragonard had imagined he was back there until the complete view through the ancient slotted window showed him the differences.

Mountain peaks, low but sharp, ranged in the near distance past the fortress walls. The triple moons shed white light into a large compound below the window. Dragonard saw half a building from his vantage point. It was a smooth bubble of chrome steel rising out of the compound's dirt.

Shiny and modern, the bubble structure made the bleakness of mortared stone all the more anachronistic. A long-staved torch planted in the dirt outside the bubble showed him two men in nondescript white uniforms. One touched the bubble's side.

Instantly a hatchway slid aside and man-made artificial light spilled into the compound. The figures in white ducked inside the bubble and the hatchway closed.

A structure of contemporary design rising from the earth inside an old fort's walls? It was enough to drive a man crazy with uncertainty—

Any man, that is, save Dragonard. A moment before seeing the unusual, unnerving sight outside, he had opened his eyes on the peg-bed and realized he was alive.

Alive . . . in possession of all of his limbs . . . and free of pain except for a faint itch around the scar-line on his scalp.

"Who gave me a new brain?" he asked. "Not that I believe you."

"I didn't expect you would right off." Jeremy chuckled, tucking the mirror's handle into his broad belt. "It was done by some of those men in the plain uniforms you saw a minute ago. It was a near thing, getting you back here with some life left in you. There's an operating theater underground—not a large one. Most of the transplant work is done elsewhere. On the various worlds where the—parts go."

Jeremy gave a sour accent to his last words. Dragonard didn't understand but did not question immediately, too shocked and thankful to disturb anything for a moment or two. Jeremy went on.

"The technicians here are highly competent. And all of the original staff except two switched over and joined the Heart Flag when I occupied this place several months ago. The two who remained loyal to the Lords—well, I gave them a chance. Then I killed them. Hungry?"

Dragonard found it easy to say, "I'm starved."

Jeremy walked to the great door bound in green-stained brass. "No wonder. You've had fluids but you've been out nearly two and a half weeks. Tonight, right after sundown, the technicians decided you were well enough to awaken. They injected stimulants. That explains the painless and pleasant way you woke up." Jeremy opened the door. "Bring the platter in."

A huge, thick-armed fighting man in Pentagon war harness appeared, carrying a platter with a ceramic ewer, a metal goblet and a joint of cold meat on it. He set it all down beside the bed and left as Dragonard attacked the food and drink.

Even stringy meat tasted wonderful. The wine, thin and sour commercial stuff, had the sweetness of a ceremonial banquet vintage.

"Forgive me if I sound thick-witted—"

Dragonard chewed, swallowed.

"—but—"

More gulping. His belly felt less empty.

"—I don't understand any of this."

"Of course you don't." Jeremy sat on a low wood stool, one leg crossed over the other. His blue eyes sparkled in the dimness. "I promised to explain the Heart Flag. Now, I think, with a new brain and spinal column and a new network of nerves, you won't merely understand; you'll appreciate what the Heart Flag is all about."

"Replacing brains?" Dragonard drained the goblet to its bottom. "Impossible."

"Why do you say that?"

"Because—because it can't be done! If it ever existed at all, the technology was lost in the wars ten thousand and more years ago."

"Lost to the many, not to the few."

"Look, Jeremy. My brain was damaged from birth. I had these—call them red periods. I'd kill people without wanting to do it. I asked my chief, Valk, the Sectioner, to put in for medical assistance for me. I wanted an operation—anything that would help. The request went all the way up to the Lords of the Exchange and it was denied. The Lords said the technology didn't exist."

"For the common man, it doesn't." Jeremy's tone remained calm but his eyes had started to burn.

"God damn you, talk straight out to me!"

Dragonard struggled off the bed, afraid his legs would betray him. But they felt as strong as ever. He went to the slot window. On the ramparts, HeartFlag warriors with spears paced. Nearer, the immense steel bubble glared in the moon, vaguely frightening in the midst of mountain-locked walls of primitive stone. Dragonard's gesture spoke eloquently of his uncertainty as it swept in everything outside.

"What is this place? Start with that."

"A very old fortress called Kalrath, in the mountains, inside the ring of electroguns."

"And here—here, on a planet where fighting men travel on four-footed creatures—you mean to tell me there's technology to rip out a man's brain and spine and replace them? Without him feeling pain afterward? There's that kind of skill here when it doesn't exist anywhere else in II Galaxy?"

"I mean to tell you exactly that, Max. It exists here and nowhere else because the Lords want it that way."

"So they'll have the benefit to themselves?"

"Exactly."

"You're lying." The whole understructure of Dragonard's world, everything he'd been taught since birth, weakened with spreading, dangerous cracks. He reacted with the anger of a man whose whole being has been threatened. "There is *no* technology to do it!"

Jeremy gazed at him steadily. "Isn't there? The technicians drilled into your head. They lifted out a huge slab of bone. They subjected your brain to the machines and discovered the apparently hereditary defect which resulted in your being a berserker. They memory-banked your stored mental impressions—please don't ask me for a technical lecture; I don't know the ins and outs—and they replaced part of your brain—"

"With *what?*"

"With part of another brain. A brain artificially synthesized from chemical materials."

"Brains *manufactured?*"

"Yes. The Lords want people to believe that technology is lost too."

"Where did the"—a wild, helpless gesture again—"spare parts come from?"

"The organ bank. There are miles and miles of storage facilities under Fortress Kalrath. Cave tunnels lined with tanks of fluid—you'll see them, don't worry. Floating in the fluid are human organs, artificial but perfect. A thousand kidneys. A thousand gall bladders. A thousand stomachs. A thousand spines. Why, the job on you was simple, Max. They could have outfitted you with ten other new parts in the theater in the dome and it would hardly have been a night's work."

Now a hurt began at the bridge of Dragonard's nose. He emptied the ewer into the goblet and drained the wine. This was worse than dying. This was lunacy.

Jeremy began to speak again, low and earnestly. The great door squealed before he'd finished one sentence and Bel slipped into the chamber. A scarlet color climbed in her cheeks as she caught sight of Dragonard sitting on the bed's edge, hunched forward, agonized, disbelieving.

She looked quite beautiful in a dove-gray tunic that reached to just above her knees and was belted in by a length of gold-plated link chain. Her breasts stood out sharply. She couldn't quite conceal her joy at seeing Dragonard alive.

Dragonard turned back to Jeremy. "Start over. Start with what you just said."

"Fortress Kalrath was established thousands of years ago, Max. It happened at the time when the Lords picked themselves out of the ruins of the war. They discovered, among other assets of the corporations which they seized, a highly refined medical technology. This they decided to keep to themselves. They did it largely because restrictions of the knowledge would enable them to hold power more firmly, making it seem to the general populace of II Galaxy that they were specially endowed, virtually ageless. To this day, Kalrath has remained the secret work-place of the scientific team most necessary to the longevity of the Lords. Only a handful of men—

two hundred, maybe, in all of II—know that Kalrath exists and what its purpose is. That purpose, simply, is to maintain and replenish the supply of synthetic organs for the Lords. When the Lords fall victim to human ills, the diseased or maimed parts of their bodies—or minds—are replaced."

Dragonard's tongue licked at his dry, cracked-open lips. "The star kings live centuries—"

"By artificial means. While ordinary people perish."

"Why was the organ bank put here?"

"Just because Pentagon was—and remains—a wild, primitive planet, with only barbarians for its home-born. The munitions works help keep it underpopulated and underdeveloped too. The way my father told it to me was that this—"

"Your *father?*"

"Mine and Bel's. He was a senior technician in the dome. I'll get to it presently. Before the wars, artificial organ synthesis as well as brain and organ transplant were highly developed technologies, used for the good of everyone. The star kings found it to their advantage to pretend that kind of knowledge never existed. Restricting it to their personal use, they made themselves seem a little closer to gods. That's what the Heart Flag is fighting against—that kind of falsehood, that kind of treachery; that kind of private power—and the obscenity of a life-saving science turned into a device to keep tottering old men on planetary thrones."

The Lords of the Exchange? Could they be responsible for such abominations? Dragonard's mind yelled in doubt—

Until he remembered the red scars on his own head.

Little seeds of belief and hate broke up, cracking the hard ground of a lifetime's faith. He said, "Go on."

"Our father," Jeremy nodded at Bel, who was listening attentively. "Our father was a technician here, as I told you. Paid well, a brilliant man. But in middle age he came to see the evil of this work and he rebelled. He was killed shortly after he admitted at a hearing that the Lords of the Exchange had become repugnant to him. The technicians turned Bel and me out into the desert, figuring starvation would finish us. I was ten, Bel was eight. Father imported a bride late in life. She died in child-bearing—a stillborn brother of ours. She wasn't allowed use of the facilities here." Jeremy's mouth wrenched. "Not even my father would have been allowed. Only the Lords. That's what began to turn him against this place."

"Obviously the desert didn't do you in."

"No, one of the wild tribes adopted us. When I was of legal age to claim my father's money from the Federated Creditbanc on Alpha Mu, I began to train the tribes and recruit from off-world. I formed the Heart Flag. A year ago this winter, we attacked Kalrath, and killed the small garrison and those two technicians I mentioned. Now we're besieged. It's a tenuous balance but it hasn't tipped in their favor."

"You mean the Lords?"

"Yes. And those who serve them, like the High Commander."

"He knows about this place?"

"Certainly. He serves the Lords. He's one of the relatively few who know."

"And that's why the electroguns faced inward! To keep the secret from getting out—"

"—and starting a rebellion under the Heart Flag. Do you notice how its symbol is designed to drive men like your High Commander crazy? A field red as human blood and in the middle, a heart of crystal full of golden wires. Artificial. It makes them froth like dogs because it says, *We know. We know and soon everyone else will too.*"

"And that's all you want?" Dragonard asked. "To bring this technology into the open?"

"Yes. To make the star kings admit what they have, and share."

Dragonard searched the younger man's face. "Do you honestly think you can?"

Now Bel spoke, strong-voiced: "We'll die before we stop trying, Dragonard."

"I can believe that."

"Do you believe the rest of it?" Jeremy wanted to know.

Dragonard thought back to Jonas Valk, to St. Anne and Mishubi II and the way they'd balked him, fought him, tried to block and trap him to prevent his coming here.

Dragonard nodded.

And in the wake of belief came an intense hatred of the whole conniving pack of those who knew, including the very Lords themselves.

Strangely, though, no red mist curled at his mind's fringes.

They let me lose my mind time after God damn time. And kill. They could have cured me if the secrets hadn't been reserved for their private use. Instead they locked me on Rankor.

He believed, and wanted to join the Heart Flag, and said so.

Jeremy laughed, clipped, short. "Max, I'm finally sure of you."

Eager for details, Dragonard asked, "What's the situation now?"

"Standoff," Bel told him. "We have Kalrath, which they need. They besiege us, uncertain."

"And the star kings, bless them," Jeremy added, "are dying for lack of transplants."

The last puzzle-bit dropped into its twisted place. Dragonard nodded.

"Strategically they're hamstrung," Jeremy continued. "We occupy Kalrath yet they can't really mount a force and destroy us. Overwhelming us would be simple, save one thing: they know we'd raze the organ banks and the dome as we went down. The Lords can't afford the loss of such precious stocks. This is the only facility of its kind in II Galaxy. In their desire for secrecy over the centuries, they neglected to take one important step: setting up an alternate bank. So we have them"—Jeremy fisted his hand—"but in a way they have us too. You know the risks involved, just keeping the place provisioned and the mercenaries paid."

"What are you going to do?" Dragonard asked.

"Wait."

"For what?"

"For them to negotiate. Rather, surrender. They

will eventually if we're strong enough and can hold out." Jeremy rose from the stool and hitched up his belt. "I remember my father. I'm strong enough to wait. I want them to agree to spread the technology. They can do it gradually; they can save face. I'll negotiate to hold Kalrath, while they *discover* the technology and make regal, ringing pronouncements and emphasize their own good works and high motives. But until every adult and child in II Galaxy can be reborn medically the same way the Lords are reborn, I'll hold Kalrath and destroy it the minute there's any treachery."

From the ramparts a watchman hallooed the hour. Another watchman replied. The voices echoed up and down the peaks. The moons silvered Bel's legs where she stood, lovely beside her brother.

"We're glad the technicians could help you, Dragonard," she said.

For the first time, a laugh came. "So it's not *policeman* any more?"

Bel's eyes were steady, with no concealment of the warmth she felt. He wished he found her as lovely as Kristin. Bel said, "Are you still a policeman? That's the crux of it."

"No." He laughed again. "No, I guess I belong to the Heart Flag now."

"You're damn right," Jeremy growled, his smile breaking all over his face.

A week passed, then another. Dragonard rode with Jeremy and Bel into the remote northwest on a recruiting swing. They fetched back two dozen young men of Pentagon, young spear-carriers with the shoulder-length hair who rode back to Kalrath chuckling in their throats at the thought of being blooded.

Dragonard rode out again to rendezvous with a swag-bellied food-runner at the electrogun ring. Two days after that, he and Jeremy and six others met the pair of black-hulled skysleds that touched down twenty miles due north on the edge of the mountain range.

And Dragonard went underground.

He toured the incredible, dimly lighted tunnels where the crystal cylinders spread into the distance along both tunnel walls. Drifting and bobbing, pairs of human-configured lungs swam like strange fish in pale pink fluid. On another level, beautifully synthesized ropes of human gut were stored, one coil to a storage tube. Each tube had a height of four feet and there were hundreds of tubes along either wall of the tunnel.

Altogether, two dozen tiers of tunnels were cut out of the rock beneath Kalrath. These weird, echoing places contrasted sharply with the bright, metal-winking quarters occupied by the technicians just under the dome. Dragonard had never seen an operating theater before and marveled.

Late in the third week, about midmorning, a rider thundered into the compound. Horns blew. Dragonard had risen late. He left the long trestle table in the main hall and ran outside. Jeremy was already there, hanging onto the rider's tether rope and listening.

"—about three hundred of them, Captain. Mounted. Also a command egg."

Jeremy whipped round as Dragonard arrived. "There are Regulators coming."

"They fired daylight shells," the rider went on.

"What color?" Jeremy asked.

"White, Captain. White as the moons, and showering all over the sky even in daylight."

Jeremy whooped. Bel arrived. He grabbed her waist and spun her high.

"White shells! The truce flare. They want to talk. We've broken them! And sooner than I thought."

Dragonard scuffed a boot in the compound earth. Suspicion nagged him.

He said nothing.

XIX

FROM THE foothills of the peaks facing south, Jeremy, Bel and Dragonard surveyed the enemy.

On the sand plain perhaps a mile away, the Regulator host had dismounted. Men loitered, smoked, their shadows reaching long and spindly over the sand in the sunset. Dragonard saw quite a few unshaven faces. St. Anne was employing mercenaries again.

Slightly to the rear of the line of men and beasts gleamed the command egg with St. Anne's pennon fluttering from the mast. A hatch stood open in the egg's side. A pole-and-cloth canopy shielded this entrance from the harsh, red sundown light flooding the Waste.

In the rocks up behind him Dragonard heard boot-scuffs and the clink of weapons. The twenty-man force Jeremy had brought along positioned itself.

"Three hundred was a close estimate," Jeremy agreed. His beast shifted under him. He patted its neck and studied the host.

Dragonard saw no point in raising the mercenary

issue. Instead he said, "Remember that's about twice what we have left. The electroguns. Get the flare going, Bel." The young man swung to slap Dragonard's shoulder. "Because they sold you out you're full of sourness. I don't blame you. But the High Commander himself shot up a white shell. That's a victory, Max. It can't mean anything else. Maybe you'd have preferred a victory in blood, but—"

Bridling, Dragonard interrupted. "That isn't it. I simply don't trust them."

Jeremy's blue eyes chilled. "I intend to hear what they have to say. Bel?"

Bel flashed Dragonard a quick glance which said she shared his suspicions. She loaded the flare-pistol, an antique with a funnel muzzle, raised the gun and pulled the trigger.

A low whistling rose away from them. Brilliant white star bursts appeared, stuttering, up in the wine-colored sky.

On the plain, the mercenaries in frayed old Regulator uniforms mounted and hauled out their weapons. Two figures emerged from the command egg, followed by a third. Jeremy jogged his beast forward. Dragonard went second in line, Bel last.

Armor covering the jutting belly of the second man under the canopy reflected the blood-ball of the sun on the horizon. Dragonard and Jeremy recognized the man's general build, his squatness, and his snowy cloak at the same time.

"That's Mishubi," Dragonard said.

Jeremy flushed with delight. "You see? One of

their very own has come to negotiate. We've won, Max. By God we have."

Reckless, Jeremy let out a yell and booted his beast into a gallop. Dragonard and Bel hurried to catch up. Dragonard's left hand hovered close to the blaster stuffed into his wide belt.

The mercenaries nudged their beasts to one side to form a lane and Jeremy and his companions galloped up it. All saffron skin and shimmering armor, Mis-hubi II stumped forth from underneath the canopy. St. Anne followed, his thin white fingers toying with a dress dagger hanging in a gold-chained scabbard at his left hip. Even though a stiff wind blew, St. Anne's thin, shining black hair hugged his skull like a cap.

The riders were halfway down the lane when St. Anne recognized Dragonard. Surprise showed, followed by outright anger. This the High Commander brought under control, but he couldn't quite damp the rage that lingered in his eyes.

Jeremy reined in. Bel and Dragonard sat their beasts just to the rear. Dragonard didn't move. His senses moved instead, catching subtle shiftings: the thud of a beast's claw-pad; the whick of a blaster control being switched over; whispers. In case things went bad, the ersatz Regulators were surrounding them.

Ebullience had Jeremy actually smiling. "Greetings, Excellences."

St. Anne touched at his upper lip. It shone with sweat. "We come in peace. But we've come to deal with the Heart Flag leader, boy."

"I'm the one known as Methuselah. My real name is Jeremy Lynx."

Thomas St. Anne's eyes flickered, remembering. "Lynx? Great God, we had you in Starmarch—"

"As a beggar on a minor offence. Yes, High Commander."

Mishubi II slid his black ball-bearing eyes toward St. Anne. The thick lips jeered. "Another splendid performance on your part." St. Anne went scarlet.

Mishubi stumped forward on his stocky legs and poked a yellow finger at Dragonard. "You I remember too. Both of you got away, am I not right? Well, we are not here to exercise punitive justice. You, youngster, look like a ragged dog. But it seems you have what we of the Exchange must have. You have it bottled up in Kalrath—"

"And won't turn it over to you for your personal use again," Jeremy said.

"You'd let us kill you, eh?"

"Yes, but more important, we'll destroy the organ banks if you try. I have men there now. There are runners up in those foothills. At the first sign of trouble the word will pass back to the Fortress. What you came for will be blown up."

Mishubi II heaved in a deep breath. "Didn't I tell you this would be their strategy, High Commander? These are not witless men. Witless men could not have outwitted such an august, clever personage as yourself all these months. What do you say, High Commander?"

Coloring, St. Anne slapped his gauntlets once against his thigh. "Of course I agree, Excellence."

Dragonard slouched in his saddle. His mouth drooped, sour. Charade?

"What's your price on Kalrath?" Mishubi rumbled. "Too many of the Lords are dying for lack of proper replacement organs. I am empowered to negotiate. Let's not waste the evening in circumlocutions and verbal fencing. Tell me straight out what you demand, boy. I have the authority to say yes or no." He paused. "The full authority of the Lords of the Exchange. Let me hear your terms."

Jeremy couldn't conceal his grin. Obviously he'd rehearsed this little scene many times.

"First I demand guaranteed amnesty, permanently documented, for all of my men."

Mishubi II sucked his fat lower lip. "Not unreasonable. Agreed. What else?"

"If we admit you to Kalrath, we will keep our personnel in the organ banks."

"You mean that we will not have direct access to the banks?"

"Not for a period of five years."

Mishubi grunted again. "A clever lad for lowborn. All right. Is that everything?"

"No. This is the most important. The technology must be spread, given back to all the people of II. I don't care how you do it. I don't care how many propaganda bulls the Lords issue to save face and announce their wonderful new discoveries. But one way or another the marvels of Kalrath have got to be shared." Jeremy leaned forward in the saddle. "That, I repeat, is the one vital condition."

St. Anne exclaimed, "It can't be met! The Lords would never agree—"

"I am negotiating for the Lords!" Mishubi thundered. "Boy, what you have just said is easy to ask and complicated to work out. I must, however, agree in principle."

Jeremy turned white. He looked as though he were going to reel out of the saddle. He held himself up, listening, as Mishubi went on.

"I am compelled to agree because the Lords are fearful of dying. But we will have to draw up a document, an agreement, a plan for getting done what you demand. You've won your battle; we might just as soon conduct the rest of our negotiations as civilized men. I suggest we retire to Kalrath, considering the matter fully negotiated in principle. Over food and a little wine we may work out the details of how the knowledge can be released without embarrassment to the Exchange."

Don't, Dragonard wanted to say. *Don't let them through the walls, Jeremy.*

"A hundred of your men can ride in, no more," Jeremy said. "The rest stay here."

Mishubi uttered a sound something like, "Uhh." He bobbed his head and called for a beast.

Expostulating in a whisper, St. Anne followed the young star king away. With an impatient wave of his chunky saffron hand, Mishubi bade the High Commander stop complaining.

Jeremy squeezed his sister's arm and grinned. Bel smiled in a wan way.

Jeremy headed his beast up the lane. Dragonard was about to follow when he noticed someone watching from the shadows inside the command egg hatch. The dark-cloaked figure stepped down under the canopy. Dragonard hauled his beast up short.

"My God. Kristin."

She leaned forward, as though to run to him. Her face was pale, without any touch of artificial coloring. Her blue eyes welled with tears.

"You're alive after all," she whispered.

Dragonard's gold eyes smoldered red in the sundown. "And finally on the right side."

"I'm working as the High Commander's aide. I had to come."

"Of course you know what the Lords have been hiding inside Kalrath for years. Or do you?"

"I found out after we left Starmarch."

"And it doesn't alter your feelings for St. Anne?"

"All my life I've been trained in loyalty—"

"And you were never sold out the way I was." Grudgingly, he nodded. "All right. I can understand that. What I don't understand is whether we're being gulled all over again."

"I listened to their conversations on the journey out here, Dragonard. Mishubi vows he speaks for all the Lords. St. Anne is against negotiating but Mishubi is in control. The Lords are tired of dying."

Dragonard's voice dropped down in his throat. "We'll find out about that, I suppose."

"Please—don't turn away like that. Can't I—let me talk to you. In the Fortress."

Dragonard wanted to say no. Then he realized he was only torturing himself, and her, for reasons that no longer existed. Mishubi II had come in good faith. And he wanted—

"Yes." A tightness in him broke. He felt joy. "Yes, Kristin. Tonight." He wheeled the beast and rode, carrying with him the bright vision of her face.

Wrong side or not, he loved her. He'd love her until the last part of him rotted in some grave somewhere.

Jeremy rode far ahead, going toward the foothills at a thundering clip. He wigwagged his arms to his watchers in the rocks. Bel took a slower pace. Dragonard caught up with her. Behind them on the plain, Mishubi and St. Anne were organizing their smaller host of a hundred.

"Are you pleased, Bel?"

"My brother's eager for this truce." She said it with a faint tone of reproof.

Dragonard studied her. For all of Bel's savage, long-legged beauty, he saw nothing but the surface of her. Everything inside him burst and shone with Kristin's face. Only Kristin's.

"I hope not too damn eager," he replied.

"You think it's more treachery?"

"I just don't know, Bel."

"We have them caught. We have what the Lords so desperately need."

"I suppose. I'm probably suspicious because of what they did to me before Jeremy had them on their knees. Still, I'm going to take steps back at Kalrath, organize as many small bands as we can spare without being noticed. Send them into the organ-bank tunnels tonight, armed. Only just in case."

Bel's brows quirked together. "Jeremy won't agree—"

"Jeremy won't know."

Bel hesitated, frowning. Then she gave a nod that agreed, and galloped ahead toward the foothills.

In the main hall of Kalrath chemical torches shed a brilliant, festive glare. Trestle tables formed parallel rows in front of the highest table. There, Jeremy sat between Mishubi II and Thomas St. Anne.

The night was well advanced. One of the mercenaries in Regulator uniform had brought a small hand-drum when he rode in; a member of the Heart Flag army had produced a cheap flute. In a show of camaraderie, the two musicians lounged on frayed cushions near the main table. Their ragged music added to the general din.

Mishubi II had fetched in several hermetic flagons of wine and crates of preprocessed meat-joints. A kind of feast of peace had been in progress for several hours. St. Anne weaved on his stool at the high table, looking thoroughly drunk. Mishubi II bent his head to listen to a remark of Jeremy's. His face split open, full of perfect white teeth.

Three hundred years old, thought Dragonard. *And kept that way at a high price. Remember, Jeremy.*

In the midst of the shouting, the laughter, the earnest conversation between Mishubi and Jeremy, Dragonard had difficulty justifying his suspicions. He had taken his precautions; he'd organized his teams and sent them—grumbling—into the tunnels. Forty-eight men were not missed as the drunkenness grew more pronounced.

Bel sat to Dragonard's right. She picked up a wine-jar as if to pass it. Dragonard shook his head, brooding.

Damn, why did every extra drop he drank leave him more sober than before?

A smell of meat and liquor breathed over the high old stone walls of the Kalrath hall. But Dragonard smelled treachery like a separate stink. His hands tingled, cold. Was it his own unslaked wish for revenge making him so distrustful? Was it only that?

Thomas St. Anne stumbled to his feet, pulled out his dress dagger and hacked a hunk of meat from a joint on a platter. Flourishing the knife, he ate the meat.

Then he waved for attention, the blade in his hand careening crazily back and forth through the air. Mishubi II ducked his head and shoved St. Anne's knife-arm aside, not without a trace of anger.

St. Anne lurched and nearly fell over. He muttered an apology to the Lord, then proceeded to gesture with the knife again, until silence rippled out over the hall.

"Clear those central tables! Clear them, I say! In honor—"

St. Anne belched. Men roared.

"—of the festivity of the occasion, of agreements amiably concluded, I have prevailed upon one of my staff members to—to entertain us with a—"

St. Anne blinked, bobbing his head. Drunk as a hen. St. Anne apparently couldn't remember what his staff member would do, so he swallowed a few more words. Finally he exclaimed:

"—to entertain us." Flourishing the knife which shone like fire, he sat down.

The hand-drum hammered; the flute wailed. Through a draped arras twisted a gleaming body.

Bells jangled and Kristin whirled into the area between the tables. She was naked except for the leather straps bearing the bells. She wore no mask this time. Her yellow hair trailed behind her like a banner.

Both affronted and fascinated, Dragonard watched. Men licked their lips. He wanted to smash their faces.

Whirling, whirling, Kristin danced past him. The tiny bells tinkled and shivered.

St. Anne lurched up again, knife still in hand. Kristin's dance carried her out in a wide circle around the rim of the cleared space. As she closed the circle, dancing back toward the high table, St. Anne shouted.

"Here! Here, lovely! Dance a little closer to the Lord so he can see—"

Reaching for her, St. Anne lost his balance. He sprawled across the table with a cry. His knife arm twisted, shot out as he fell. The dress dagger he'd been flourishing glared. Dragonard howl-raged to his feet to warn her as the wild momentum of Kristin's dance carried her blindingly on, straight onto the outflung point of St. Anne's knife.

The knife went hilt-deep in her naked belly. Kristin stiffened. Her blue eyes turned wild with fright as she stared down, impaled. The hand-drum beat twice more, stopped.

Jeremy leaped up. So did everyone else. Dragonard overturned his table, charging toward her. At last Kristin realized what had happened. Blood poured down her legs and she screamed.

XX

KRISTIN'S SCREAM trailed off into the kind of moan that signaled a faint. Kneeling, Dragonard caught her. He tried to cradle her gently. Blood purled from her wound, spread down across her bare hip to leak sticky-warm onto his leg. All the color drained from her skin. In her nakedness she looked small and fragile.

Dragonard's head lifted. Mishubi's face registered consternation, concern. The dreadful silence clung in the hall until St. Anne whispered an oath. He wiped at the corners of his dulled eyes.

"Accident," he said. "God save me, too much to drink—I swear I didn't mean—"

Mishubi II drove his palm against the shoulder of a stunned Jeremy. "Go see what can be done for her. This is Kalrath, after all."

Jeremy shook himself like a pup coming from water. He vaulted the table, knelt beside Dragonard. Mishubi berated St. Anne.

"It seems you apply a clumsy touch to everything, High Commander. I have no patience with a man who will permit wine to dull his mind."

"Excellence, I swear it was unintentional!"

"Is she breathing?" Mishubi called down.

Jeremy drew back to let Dragonard lean his cheek near Kristin's mouth. A faint warmth brushed against his skin.

"Barely."

"We'll go to the dome." Jeremy stood. "Can you carry her, Max?"

Dragonard nodded. Ever so slowly, he unbent his knees. Kristin lay back in his arms. The leather strap fell off her neck. The bells jangled wildly as Jeremy caught the strap and flung it away. Dragonard started across the hall, walking slowly, with even steps.

Mishubi II clumped from the high table and St. Anne followed, half complaining, half sobbing. Dragonard saw only fragmentary details of everything around him. Mishubi's gold thumb ring with the blood-colored stone flashed as the Lord of the Exchange bellowed to those in the hall:

"All remain. The feast may continue. But without laughter or singing."

A door opened and night wind fanned his face. Jeremy ran ahead through the gently blowing dust of the compound. At the dome he pressed his hand against the metal surface and the hatchway hissed out of the way.

Jeremy stood to one side. Dragonard turned sideways to make the passage easier with Kristin sprawled out in his arms.

Several of Mishubi's men emerged from the fortress door on the other side of the compound. The Lord of the Exchange, who was halfway to the dome, raised his voice, ordering them to return inside. Dragonard ducked into the dome and down a moving spiral belt which carried him and his burden to the level below.

The walls of the dome shimmered with non-glare white light. Tonight the brilliance seemed sterile, unfeeling. So did the bland-faced technician who emerged from a cubicle. On the level above, Mishubi could be heard still chastising St. Anne as the moving spiral belt lowered them.

"She's one of the Lord's party," Jeremy said to the technician. "Stabbed by accident."

The technician examined Kristin quickly. "That's very nasty."

"Which diagnostic machine do you want to use?" Jeremy asked.

"The larger, I think." The technician turned. "This way."

A featureless section of wall shot upward into hidden grooves as the technician approached. Beyond, complicated apparatus of bright metal and glass was ranged over the floor of a small circular chamber. The technician flipped console switches and a pedestal rose from the floor.

Leaves unfolded from the pedestal's top to form a platform. The technician pulled down a long flexible hose from a hanging hook and flicked a stud on the nozzle, spraying back and forth. The plastic foamed out gray, hardening instantly to form a resilient cushion which covered the entire platform. The technician hung up the hose and rolled the hook out of the way on its overhead trolley.

"Rest her there, please. The cushioning will adapt to her shape."

Gently, gently, Dragonard lowered the naked girl. Blood still ran down over her hip. It spread out through the porous cushioning, turning it dark. The technician was joined by another. The second man spoke in a whisper to the first, who nodded. The second technician hurried to a larger console and started whirling dials.

A section of the curved chamber wall opened and another device rolled out, suspended by microthin cables from the trolley. The device resembled an oversized cathode-ray tube. The first technician caught it, positioned it just above Kristin's middle.

"Ready," he said. "Give me the display."

The second technician threw controls in sequence. An oblong area of the ceiling lighted; onto it a pattern leaped. Dragonard saw an unfamiliar intestinal geography illuminated in tones of gray. He heard a light clink behind him and turned.

St. Anne stood near the entrance, partly shielding Mishubi II. The clink sounded again as Mishubi shifted his balance.

Had the Lord been wearing a dress sword at the banquet? Dragonard tried to remember. He couldn't see Mishubi's right side, blocked as the Lord was by St. Anne in front of him. Mishubi was concentrating on Kristin's floodlit body.

Had that been a scabbard-clink? Where had Mishubi gotten a sword? Why would—?

A hand seized Dragonard's arm. He started. It was only Jeremy, who pointed to the flickering display screen high above them.

At various points on the living radiograph, small colored circles had lit. Bulbs of the corresponding color flashed on and off the face of the larger console. The second technician indicated each in turn.

"Substantial hemorrhaging here and here. The orange light indicates the lower bowel. It's completely severed."

The first technician rubbed his forehead. "She won't live long as she is." The man obviously recognized the Lord of the Exchange from his ceremonial armor. Nervously he added, "Are we authorized to—?"

"I'm still in charge of Kalrath," Jeremy interrupted. "Of course you're authorized to do a transplant."

The technician nodded. He said to his assistant, "Run me a part number check, please."

Moving to a small disc-shaped computer, the other technician programmed the request. On the spiral belt a shadow appeared. Bel's legs revolved into sight, then all of her. Dragonard wasn't thinking too clearly, but his mind functioned well enough to register the sight of a blaster tucked into Bel's belt. The weapon was partially concealed by a fold of her dove-colored robe. *Good.*

He turned back to the table. Kristin's breasts barely moved with life-breath.

The computer coughed, clicked and spat out three inches of tape which the technician ripped off. He read the punchcode aloud: "Code 202. The ninth level."

"But you'll have to hurry," the first technician cautioned. "She's losing blood fast."

"I'll go for it," Jeremy said. "They have to be brought up by hand."

"Let me go with you," Dragonard said.

Bel's face tightened with the pain she felt for Dragonard. She gave a small nod and touched her belt, as if to say she understood Dragonard's concern, and that she could watch Mishubi II and St. Anne. The latter weaved on his feet, staring at absolutely nothing.

Jeremy's boots hammered as he ran. "Gravtube this way."

The theater wall slid aside at his touch. An aseptic tunnel, dimly lighted, ran down to a wider loading area for a pair of tubes. Jeremy stepped into the right-hand one. Dragonard was right behind.

Moments later they stepped out onto the rocky floor of the ninth storage level of the underground organ bank.

Like gently swimming eels, the coils of synthesized guts bobbed in the transparent tubes mounted in steel sockets on either side of the rock passage. Jeremy counted inventory plate numbers as they hurried along. "Two eighty-nine. Two eighty-seven—the one we want will be all the way to the end of the right-hand side. It'll take two minutes to drain the fluid level to the point where the part falls into the carrying tank. Don't worry, we'll make it."

Dragonard's mind heard only part of what Jeremy said. His boots clattered in the eerie emptiness. The bank tunnel was lighted by glow-cells affixed to the rock ceiling every twenty feet or so. Strange ceiling shadows were projected through the storage tanks onto the walls behind; shadows that curled, twisted, writhed like huge serpents.

Dragonard spotted the plate affixed to the socket base. "There. Third from the end."

Jeremy brushed past him. The storage corridor stretched away into the distance. Far down it, Dragonard saw a pair of man-shaped shadows that straightened at the clack of boots. Without thought his hand went to his blaster.

Then he remembered the teams he'd stationed underground. Jeremy didn't notice. He was busy examining the small plate of push-buttons on the face of the mounting socket.

Jeremy pushed the second button from the top. It was etched in white with the word: *Discharge*.

Bubbles raced up through the pink fluid in the tank; the fluid level began to drop.

"The diagnostic machine's a marvel," Jeremy said, talking fast and low because he saw the morbid, anguished way Dragonard watched the tank. "Makes a perfect computerized match to the most properly configured part in the bank—the part just right for the patient. Very likely this is the only part that could adapt to Kristin, too. Since the Lords come in various shapes and sizes, there are seldom two identical parts in the bank at any one time. But this will be the right one."

"The damn stuff is taking forever to drain."

Jeremy had his back to the part of the corridor where Dragonard's team waited, unmoving. Jeremy started to reply. Then his face bleached.

"Down!" he bawled, and hit Dragonard in the belly with his shoulder.

Dragonard crashed into a storage tank across the way. A blaster pared the air where he'd been.

The tank containing Code 202 shattered and pink liquid spilled out onto the rock floor. The synthetic intestines were sloshed out along with it.

Sprawled, Jeremy shoved himself up by his hands. The blaster beam crisped the glistening intestines to nothing. And from down between the tanks rolled the voice of Mishubi.

"So much for your fancy, Policeman. The young lady is expendable."

Dragonard's hand formed a claw that dropped toward his own blaster.

Pale but thoroughly sober, Thomas St. Anne stood alongside the chunky Lord. St. Anne licked his lips and switched his head from side to side in a quick, cautionary movement. His blaster hand was steady.

Dragonard's hand stayed off the blaster butt.

"You stinking bastards," he said. "Gulled after all."

Mishubi grunted. "Quite so."

Dragonard's gold eyes caught fire. He jerked his hand at the charred remains of the synthetic intestine. "Why did you have to do that? We're the ones you want."

"That is true," Mishubi returned. "The little police agent meant nothing, save a pretty means to add more pain to your punishment. She did have an eye for you, Policeman. That did not go unnoticed."

"I believed you," Jeremy said. "God steal my soul, I did."

"I knew it was wrong," Dragonard growled. "Never trust the Lords."

"Ah, but you fail to understand." Mishubi II smiled then, his saffron face cracking into all sorts of deep folds and wrinkles. His jollity was horrifyingly false. "Tonight I do not act for the Lords but for myself. For the Tychohama worlds. After this night there'll be but one center and source of power and authority in all II Galaxy. I will be that one!"

With his fisted free hand Mishubi II thudded his own armored chest. Wave on wave of apprehension and terror hit Dragonard as he saw the high-riding ambition, the almost animalistic belief in self-power shining in the up-tilted black eyes.

"Bel!" Jeremy exclaimed. "What's happening up in the theater—?"

St. Anne said, "By now your sister should be a prisoner. And your troops overwhelmed. The Lord gave the signal and shot the technicians before we descended."

"How much are you after?" Dragonard breathed.

"All of it," Mishubi replied. "All of II Galaxy, every last planet. I will take it by virtue of control of this place alone. When I have Kalrath, I have everything. I am young enough, you see, and I've hated the older ones a long time. They call me an arrogant whelp. Well, now I will control them . . . control these banks, and the life of all the Lords. I have been building mercenary legions myself since the first word of the Heart Flag drifted to my ears. Huge legions . . . hundreds of thousands. Do you know where those legions stand tonight?"

Jeremy's face mirrored only part of the enormity of the plan unfolded to them. "Where?"

"At every strategic citadel in II Galaxy. One after another, the Lords and their closest advisers will fall in palace coups. We shall observe the ceremonies, of course. The Lords won't be slaughtered; rather, they'll be permitted to die natural deaths." Mishubi II waved his blaster at the storage banks. "I'll give them none of these."

"Armies set to move?" Dragonard said. "All over II Galaxy?"

"Yes, and splendidly organized by my trusted aide the High Commander. His planning and administrative abilities are only outshone by his ambition."

St. Anne's neatly parted hair shone in the ceiling glow. "I accept the compliment, Lord."

"When will the armies strike?" Jeremy asked.

"The moment we flash word that the organ bank is in our possession," said St. Anne. "I should judge that won't be long now."

"The banquet tonight—pretending to drink too much—the accident with the knife—" Dragonard's cheeks were white as bone. "That was all a trick and a lie."

"For the sole purpose of obtaining entrance to these premises," Mishubi rumbled. "Yes."

Dragonard had no time to dwell on the staggering scope of the plan, nor on all the insane, ambition-fired convolutions of Mishubi's mind that had convinced him at some point back in time that he could pull it off. Damnably, he might. Kalrath was the whole key.

St. Anne lifted his blaster. The lightning-jag emblems on his high collar flashed.

"I think we might eliminate them now, Excellence," he murmured.

"Yes, we'll want to see to affairs aboveground."

St. Anne's finger tightened on the blaster's control. "This gives me a good deal of pleasure, Dragonard. You have always been a filthy, arrogant—"

Mishubi II cried a warning.

He hauled the snowy cloak around him and hurled himself against the storage cylinder on his left. A blaster beam sizzled past Dragonard's shoulder and smoked the air where the Lord had been.

St. Anne yelped and dodged, stumbling backward. Dragonard heard running boots as his team came up the corridor from the position they'd crept to. Both men opened up with their blasters but running, their aim was poor. They both missed.

St. Anne pushed Mishubi down the corridor toward the gravtubes. Jeremy's blue eyes flared. The two Heart Flag men pounded up. One growled: "We heard that talk of killing you and decided to open up."

"Where did these men come from?" Jeremy demanded.

"I put them down here, and others in the other tunnels. I smelled a trick. There go the fish into the gravtube. We'd better get after them."

The men ran single file. Dragonard tried to thrust Kristin's face from his mind, tried to remember what this moment meant.

If they lived to reach aboveground, they'd probably find chaos, and the last battle for Kalrath already begun.

XXI

AT THE GRAV TUBES Jeremy barred the Up entrance by flinging his arm across it.

"Let me listen a second."

He cocked his head. Then: "All quiet up there. Damn odd. Mishubi and St. Anne must have reached the dome. Theoretically they should be storming it."

"Dammit, let's go up," Dragonard said. "Kristin's going to die unless—"

"I'm more concerned about Kalrath dying." Jeremy's lips peeled back as he spewed out the words. Dragonard could almost feel the self-hate in them; Jeremy had accepted the bargainers in good faith. "How many have we got stationed in the tunnels?"

"Forty-eight," Dragonard answered. "Two in each of the two dozen tunnels."

With a nod Jeremy signed to the pair of fighters who'd saved them from assassination. "One of you take the Up tube as soon as we leave. The other one take the Down tube now. Alert the men on each level. Tell them to get into a position near the tube entrance on their level. We'll try to send reinforcements down right away. I don't like that damn silence. Come on, Max." He leaped and the reverse field levitated him up the tube.

Floating swiftly up beneath him, Dragonard held his blaster tight. The levels dropped away under them. From overhead dim sounds of fighting became audible. Men yelled, blasters hissed. Over it all was a counterpoint of clanking metal, swords on swords. Dragonard's heart raced so fast it hurt inside his chest. He tried to hold his fury and fear in check.

Jeremy stepped off the tube at the main loading area. He waited for Dragonard. The men crept down the short passage into the theater. Jeremy whipped through the door, stepping out to the right and covering the place with his blaster. Dragonard jumped behind him, going left.

Their weapons covered silence, a thin smoke, death.

"Oh, God," Dragonard said. He ran forward. "Kristin."

On the diagnostic platform, Kristin lay without moving. He touched her bloodied hip. The blood came away faintly congealed. He rolled her right eyelid back and bit down on his bottom lip. Disfigured by the browning wound, she seemed carved out of smooth white stone. He was hit by the stinging awareness of how soft and mortal she'd been.

He whirled around. Jeremy peered up the spiral belt-stair. It had stopped, buckling in several places, and smoke was seeping from the jammed rollers underneath. The two technicians lay on the floor, both dead. One had no head left.

Dragonard ripped off a part of the man's white coverall and covered as much of Kristin's body as he could. For a moment his eyes glittered wet at the outer corners. Then the gold in them appeared to darken.

Above, the sword-clanks, the erupting blasters, the cacophony of curses and yells dinned.

"Let's go up there," Dragonard said.

Climbing like a limber cat, he reached the upper level ahead of Jeremy. The hatchway into the compound hung askew, a blast-hole blown into its center. Dragonard jumped out into the compound and threw himself sideways, away from the broad bar of light spilling across the dirt.

Out of the dark a blaster cut a stencil-line of fire; the hatchway fell all the way off. Before the unseen marksman fired again, Jeremy leaped out into the clear.

The compound was a shambles. The great outer gates had been blown off their hinges. Men fought hand to hand in the ill-lit confusion. Nearby a bearded fellow in frowsy Regulator's uniform was throttling a Pentagon warrior in fighting harness.

The warrior beat at his foe's skull with the broken butt of a spear. The Regulator bore him to the ground. Dragonard raced forward to where the two men struggled on the near edge of the seething, caterwauling mob. Hate fumed in him. Not red, but cool, lightless, devastating in its depth and cruelty. He snatched the false Regulator's hair, yanked the man's head back, thrust the muzzle of his blaster into the man's startled mouth and triggered.

In a stinking puff the head dissolved. Dragonard jumped back out of the way as the droplets of liquefied brains scattered foul-smelling on his arms and legs.

The warrior stumbled up, massaging his throat. Jeremy ranged through the edges of the struggle, bawling Bel's name.

The warrior blurted out: "They turned on us all, right at the tables—"

"These aren't all of the enemy," Dragonard broke in. "Where are the rest?"

The warrior waved up toward the jumbled battlements of Kalrath. "Gone off there someplace. I am afraid, Maxdragon. The Lord and the policeman ran out of the dome. They called many orders in an unfamiliar tongue. The fortress is surrounded but where most of the enemy inside has gone, no one knows. Perhaps to work magic spells in the dark—"

"Get that nonsense out of your head," Dragonard spat. "They're as human as we are. Jeremy?"

"Here."

Blue eyes sick with concern, Jeremy ran to his side. Behind him came Bel. She carried Jeremy's battered old horn. The Heart Flag men were doing well enough against the false Regulators in the compound. But counting both sides, no more than forty or fifty fought.

"Bel says Mishubi's other soldiers were already in position when the attack started," Jeremy said. "They rode up from the plain after dark and hid in the rocks outside the walls."

Bel's deep red hair blew fitfully around her shoulder. She fended a Regulator driven into her by the spear-lunge of a Heart Flag warrior. She sidestepped, tripping the uniformed man. The harnessed warrior howled and rammed his spearpoint into his enemy's throat. Bel turned quickly back to them.

"The Lord gave orders in some sort of oral code. Most of his followers went with him up on the battlements."

"It's like a puzzle-maze up there," Jeremy cursed. "A thousand turns and hiding places."

"The others are attacking the walls from outside," Bel rushed on. "Grapnels and ropes—"

"Mishubi can't do much damage from the battlements," Jeremy decided. He hauled up the old trumpet and blew a pair of ragged notes. His men had the situation under virtual control in the compound. Matched man for man, and with their loyalty to Jeremy to turn them to berserkers, they had murdered most of the false Regulators. In moments Jeremy had a band around him, thirty or so strong.

Heads ran with drips of blood. But there was laughter among the Pentagon men, nudging, pride in small battles well fought. Even a few of the thuggish mercenaries looked pleased.

"Ten of you stay here," Jeremy ordered. He thrust the old trumpet at one of them. "Three blasts if Mishubi returns. He'll have to enter the underground through the dome—there's no other way. We'll try to cut off the ones on the walls and round up the rest of our people. Dragonard—you and Bel go along the inner wall with five. I'll take the rest out the gates and along the other side."

The group broke, knots of silvered ghost-figures under the soaring triple moons. Bel led the way around the dome and into the shadow of the long fortress wall. Some distance ahead, Heart Flaggers fought hand to hand with a sizable enemy force up on the wide walk at the top of the wall.

Bel's boots pounded. Dragonard ran beside her. He kept twisting his head around, searching the stair-step silhouette of Kalrath's towers against the sky. He thought he saw shadow-men racing along up there but couldn't be positive.

What in damnation were Mishubi and his High Commander up to?

"Stairs ahead," Bel called in warning. The stairs led to the area of fighting atop the wall.

Dragonard pushed past her and picked off three Regulators with his blaster as he went up two steps at a time. They reached the top. Swords clanged, spears winked and sailed in the night's uncertain light. Bel slashed into the pack with her dagger and a throat above a Regulator collar fountained blood.

Below the wall on the outside, Dragonard saw Regulator uniforms by the tens and fifties. The enemy scrambled up knotted ropes which served as improvised ladders. Dragonard knelt on the parapet and aimed downward.

A Regulator uniform blurred at him from behind. He twisted, belted his fist into the running man's belly. Then he stood straight up and heaved.

The uniformed man arched out and down through the air, screaming. His head smashed a small boulder and burst. Dragonard laughed a cold laugh and began to burn through the nearest grapnel-held rope with his blaster on low beam.

The rope parted and down tumbled the climbers. Dragonard turned on full charge and directed the beam downward. The climbers died.

Men fired back at him from the other ropes to right and left. Beams smoked past his head. He hardly heard or saw; like the men of Pentagon, he'd become a berserker. He fought like a machine. No redness in his brain; no loss of powers of his senses; only a consuming, wordless desire to kill them, kill them all—

In the tangle directly below him, the last man disappeared in blaster-fire, shrieking.

From down along the right, Jeremy slipped in fast. He'd come round through the gate to get behind the climbers. Spears glared, hurled hard. A Regulator fell off a rope with his backbone impaled. Jeremy's small band fanned out along the rocks opposite the wall, setting up a withering fire from their few blasters.

Out of the noise Bel cried something. Dragonard kicked and clubbed his way toward her. He tried to follow her pointing.

The Heart Flag men chased Regulators along the battlement, catching them, slaying them. They were carrying the day there. Dragonard took heart until he saw to what Bel pointed, her face frightened.

On a far battlement circles of white light opened. "Portabeams!" Dragonard breathed. "Not hard for

Mishubi's men to carry. What's that thing the beams are focused on?"

His heart caught. He recognized the sleek, pointed cylindrical metal object pinned in the intersecting glares of the beams. Men swarmed around it.

A telescoping track shot downward into the darkness under the parapet where fifty of the enemy must be gathered. Three men lifted the sharp-pointed cylinder over onto the track. With a cough, fire sprang from the cylinder's stub rear end. It whistled down the track into the darkness point first.

A low, muffled detonation came. Then another, fainter, blending with a heavy grinding.

"Bastard," Dragonard said. "St. Anne must have stolen half the Gannonblock arsenal."

The muffled detonations continued, each seeming fainter than the last. Men on the brightly lighted battlement out of blaster-range flung ropes down. They scrambled away into the dark, following the heavy machine-like grind which rose from the place where darkness had swallowed the cylinder. Under his feet Dragonard thought he felt the wall shift ever so slightly.

"What is that thing?" Bel whispered.

"Portable bombdrill. The parts can be carried in twenty field packs and assembled in half an hour. St. Anne must have hoisted it up from around back of that wall where he's—"

Suddenly it all fell into place. Dragonard ran to the parapet where Jeremy's firepower had picked off nearly the last Regulator.

"Jeremy!" he screamed down. "They're going in

another way! They're boring in from over on the other side of the fortress!"

Jeremy's cloak flapped as he ran forward from the rocks. "What, what? I can't hear you—"

"They're making their own route into the organ bank. Going down through the earth with a bombdrill. It blows open a passage wide enough for a man to crawl through and—"

"More men coming," Bel cried. "Inside the walls—"

Dragonard wheeled back. No time to bawl to Jeremy that Mishubi II and St. Anne had abandoned the dome entrance to the underground so the Heart Flag men could be divided, chewed apart while a safe new way of entrance was found. Under the wall on the inside, figures scuttled from the direction of the dome. Dragonard began firing his blaster recklessly. The smell, the rotten smell of another trap clung in his nose.

A heaving, shining wall of fire leaped up from just inside the wall, sheeting up toward his face. He lunged for Bel, wrapped his arms around her and leaped outward.

"Stole the whole God damn arsenal—" His shout was lost in the fire-shot thunder.

Falling outward, time slowed for him. He understood their strategy: create a diversion at the outer wall; then, by erecting a flame-wall inside with portable equipment, thrust the Heart Flag defenders toward the outside and leave them sticking there like a boil above skin.

The fortress wall buckled under the blast of radiating heat from the wall of fire which leaped toward the sky for a distance of several hundred yards. Rocks rained on him. Bel dropped away. He hit the boulders outside the wall, instinctively shielded his head—

He awoke among the rocks under the triple moons, with only Jeremy and Bel and half a dozen others crouching around him. Over Jeremy's shoulder he saw what remained of Kalrath's outer wall.

It bristled with armed men in Regulator uniforms. Screams of Heart Flag soldiers still trapped inside and being slaughtered came drifting. Over everything lay the rhythmic muffled thud of the bombdrill boring down into the organ bank tunnels. Dragonard thought of the pairs of men waiting and waiting in the tunnels for reinforcements that would never arrive.

Mishubi II had won. He divided them, tricked them to the wall and pushed them outside. He created the boil and then lopped it off.

Dragonard wiped a blood-thread from the corner of his lip. He staggered up, dizzy.

"What have we got to fight with?" he asked.

Bel whispered to the few men who remained. After a moment she said, "Two blasters. A pack of thermal explosive that Neel here managed to steal from the armory. I have my dagger. Jeremy has his. You have your blaster." Her voice was empty.

"How many of us left?" Dragonard asked.

"This is all," Jeremy said. His face turned up to the moon, bright with failure and hate of himself. Dragonard wondered what had become of the red banner with its crystal heart full of golden wire. Such a brave flag.

"This is all," Jeremy repeated.

From the wall of Kalrath they heard laughter.

XXII

JEREMY PLUCKED at his cloak. He acted like a man lacking full possession of his senses. His blue eyes ran from face to face, seeming to recognize no one. Bel met Dragonard's gaze over her brother's shoulder and quickly she looked away. She was sharing Jeremy's shame.

At length Jeremy crouched down. He leaned against a chilly rock and covered his forehead and eyebrows with his right hand. A sigh whispered from him.

Dragonard had heard the sounds of men cracking before. Sometimes it was an oath, a sob, or merely a silent change in the attitude of the shoulders. Outwardly a man might remain the same, or appear so to strangers. Inside, in an instant, a whole lifetime's balance could shift. Dragonard stared at his boots. To witness such a moment was an awful experience.

"Blame me," Jeremy said. "Blame me for it all."

Bel said, "That isn't fair. You thought you'd won. We all did."

From under the shield of hand Jeremy said, "Dragonard didn't."

"A hunch, that's all," Dragonard said. "Just as easily wrong as right."

Jeremy began to swear. He cursed in desperate, filthy language. Two of the other survivors, the crook-nosed mercenary Neel one of them, moved away nervously and whispered together.

A portion of Kalrath's wall was visible just to the right of a massive, anvil-shaped rock. Dragonard studied the situation from the cover of the rock's shadow.

A good one hundred yards of the wall had been blown away. It was directly behind this jagged gape that the flame-wall had spurted up. Now the fire had been turned off. Dragonard saw indistinct figures loitering in the silver-and-shadow on the other side of the gap. No doubt the false Regulators still had the flame-wall equipment in position; it was the best way to guard the breach.

But hell, what would he be if he tried to slip into the North Waste alone, catch a freighter off Pentagon and try to start over?

Answer: zero. A man with no chances. A man Mishubi II and St. Anne would hound to the end of creation.

Besides, in his own emotionless way he'd come to believe in the Heart Flag. And the worst that could happen now, thinking of II Galaxy, would be for Mishubi to remain in control of the organ banks. Mishubi's palace coups would water away to empty victories without the banks in his possession.

Or in existence.

In the shine of the triple moons Dragonard stared at Kalrath. He decided.

He admitted to himself that he might have done nothing if there'd been a chance of a new life somewhere else. There was none. And he'd been gulled by the Lords; deceived and betrayed most of all by St. Anne and the one Lord of the Exchange who wanted all of II in his thick damn yellow hands.

Dragonard rose and signaled to Bel. She made a countersign which asked whether Dragonard wanted her to attract Jeremy's attention. Jeremy still sat motionless against the rock, eyes shielded.

With a negative shake of his head, Dragonard pointed to the mercenary Neel. Then he made a motion which said *Bring him*.

Bel left her brother. In a moment Neel crept into the concealment of the rock's looming shadow. Bel hovered behind.

"Have you got the pack of thermal with you?" Dragonard asked.

Neel nodded. He lifted a four-by-four-by-two-inch metal container from carry-prongs on his belt. "Grabbed it from the armory just before a bunch of them banged down the door. I barely got out through a slot window. I wanted to detonate this right in the middle of them. I never had time. We were called to the wall—"

"Give it to me," Dragonard said.

Bel started to say something. She saw Dragonard's bleak expression. She knew.

Dragonard stared at Bel for a long minute. His gold eyes said she had better say nothing; a flicker of emotion in her eyes indicated her fear. She understood how he felt, understood she had better not oppose him, and it frightened her. Dragonard was glad he'd communicated.

Turning the pack in his hands, he examined the numerals indicating the charge size.

"Zero-forty. That's fine. Now if there's filament enough—yes."

Using his thumbnail he broke the seal which connected the little storage tray to one end of the pack. Inside, the microthin strand glittered to a coil. The small thumb-push at one end of the filament and the jack at the other appeared undamaged.

"Bel," he said, "you get your brother and the others at least half a mile back into these rocks within five minutes. But do it without alarming them. Don't let them think there's reason for urgency. Suggest it's safer." Dragonard stared back over his shoulder at the crumbled peaks surrounding Kalrath in a wide bow. "Actually it will be."

"Jeremy wouldn't try to stop you—"

Dragonard cut her off. "I don't know what Jeremy would try. I'm not going to run any risks with a man whose whole reason for living is gone. Do what I say."

She bowed her head. It gave him little satisfaction. Once he would have relished the way she finally acknowledged his command with that gesture. It didn't matter now.

"Neel, I need one of their uniforms. You'll have

to be quiet. Take Bel's dagger and try near the gate. You may be able to pick off a man wandering too far from his post. Wait as long as you have to in order to do the job with no noise." Dragonard paused. "That is, if you're willing. Otherwise I'll go myself."

Neel wiped his nose. "I'm willing. My job's fighting. I hate to be losers."

Dragonard gave one nod. "Move out. But not in Jeremy's direction."

Bel slipped off. Dragonard unrolled the jack end of the filament and plugged it into the pack. With extreme care he hung the pack on his belt with the carry-prongs and hooked the tiny filament coil over the right prong, with the thumbpush dangling free. A touch on the push by accident and he'd be blown up.

He sat back to wait.

Shadows shifted as the moons raced on. His throat felt dry. Bel was talking with the other survivors. Dragonard heard a noise behind some rocks on his right, peered that way, saw nothing. Neel?

Looking in the other direction he discovered that Bel had already cleared the area. Of Jeremy and the rest there was no sign.

Neel slid out from a narrow crevice between two rocks. He held up a bundle and grinned.

"That didn't take long," Dragonard said as he climbed into the filthy Regulator trousers.

"They've rigged the area just outside the gates for the animals," Neel answered. "Hammered in pen wires and strung picket ropes. With the animals milling, I had an easy time. I picked off the man nearest the rocks. Half a dozen of those phony bastards—"

Dragonard said, "You spotted that, did you?"

"Back at the fight at the rock, when I saw their beards. I was at Gannonblock—I know my own kind."

"You say Mishubi's men are out among the animals?"

"Feeding ration pellets by hand. I took the nearest. Easy."

Now Dragonard had his arms into the Regulator blouse. Carefully he buttoned the front so that it concealed the pack on the carry-prongs of his belt beneath. "Did you use the knife?"

"No." Neel raised his hands and smiled with cruel joy.

Something made Dragonard laugh then. Maybe he'd live through it. Maybe. He slapped Neel on the shoulder and ordered him to search for the others in the rocks behind.

"Where are you going to put it?" Neel wanted to know.

"I'm going to walk in the gate and slap it on the dome and run the filament out again."

Neel clucked his tongue. "I heard about you before, Policeman. They called you a crazyman but they were always scared of you. Now I see why. Have luck."

Dragonard's gold eyes loomed as he stood up beside the rock. "Have luck."

Neel vanished. Dragonard cut back through the rocks, working toward the left and the gate.

It took him the better part of half an hour. He crept

with extreme caution, searching the ground ahead for ambush sites. Mishubi II might already have squads out searching for survivors.

But he ran into no resistance.

At last he reached the spot he wanted. He edged around a moon-whitened rock and flattened his spine against it.

Directly ahead of him, beasts stamped and blew softly, roped to a pin-line. Beyond that line was another, and another . . . four lines in all. Over the scaled backs of the animals Dragonard saw the shattered gates. False Regulators still moved among the shuffling animals, feeding food pills into the maws, one pill to an animal.

Taking a breath, Dragonard stepped from the rock's cover. He darted past the nearest beast, running his hand along its flank and whispering a word to soothe it. He ducked under the next picket rope and almost ran into a uniformed man.

The man swore as the beast nipped the edge of his hand in its haste to get at the pellet.

"Finished already?" the false Regulator grumbled at Dragonard.

"Right you are."

Dragonard kept moving, past the third picket rope. Another false Regulator there had completed his feeding. Dragonard paused to run a hand along the neck of a kneeling beast. The Regulator who'd finished walked back through the gates. The one uniformed man with a ray rifle stationed there hardly gave a glance.

They're sure, Dragonard thought. *So damn sure they've won.* Galling. But it helped him.

He passed through the gate with a wave; the man on duty returned his wave laconically. From the slot windows of the great hall overlooking the compound came sounds of laughter and singing. Groups of uniformed men crossed the dark compound, going about their duties. Two emerged from the torn-open door of the metal dome toward which Dragonard was headed.

Halfway there and not so much as a hail. He supposed it was because a man of Mishubi's stature and position thought in terms of massive forces, fifties and hundreds and thousands of men. Only St. Anne, really, would understand what a single police agent with nerve could do.

Dragonard blended into the shadows to the right of the dome door and unbuttoned the stolen uniform blouse. He lifted the pack off its prongs, peeled back the adhering strip and shoved the pack hard against the curve of metal.

It held.

Dragonard reached for the coil of micro-filament. He planned to go up the stone stairs just behind him to the top of the wall, stringing the filament as he went. When he reached the top he'd have to jump over and run and hope to be taken for a fugitive. The safety of the filament would be uncertain but he couldn't play it otherwise.

Just as Dragonard started to unreel the filament and back toward the steps, Thomas St. Anne walked out of the dome door.

He saw Dragonard. He took an involuntary step toward him, half in, half out of the bar of light.

Dragonard never moved faster in his life. Conscious of the thumb-push swinging wildly at his belt, he caught St. Anne's arm and jerked him out of the light. He brought his left hand up and shoved it into St. Anne's face, palm driven against St. Anne's teeth to stifle his scream, index and third fingers hooked into St. Anne's eyesockets and pulling, pulling down.

The two men teetered in the darkness. St. Anne made faint gurgling sounds. He bit into the butt of Dragonard's palm and blood spurted. Dragonard's hand burned as his fingers dragged down into St. Anne's eyeballs.

St. Anne twisted his dress dagger out of its scabbard and rammed it into Dragonard's ribs.

Dragonard fought a scream, killed it in his throat. The blade twisted in his side and struck against bone. Dragonard brought his right hand over, seizing St. Anne's wrist. The High Commander's lightning-jag emblems of office flashed and dazzled on his collar as he rocked back and forth.

St. Anne tried violently to free himself from Dragonard's double grip. Neither man made a sound louder than harsh breathing. Dragonard applied more pressure to St. Anne's wrist.

He could feel the knife blade scrape against bone inside him. He jerked his midsection backward and the blade loosened, slicing more flesh and cloth as it tore out. Dragonard bent St. Anne's wrist over harder.

Bone broke. St. Anne's knees collapsed. As the High Commander sagged, Dragonard shoved the man's knife hand hard. St. Anne's blade went in through his own spotless uniform blouse. Dragonard kept digging St. Anne's eyeballs with his other hand. The knife blade disappeared. The hilt was flush with St. Anne's uniform.

Dragonard released the hand he'd been using on St. Anne's face and whipped it to the High Commander's throat to throttle his windpipe and prevent a dying scream. For a few seconds St. Anne stared at him through thc blood weltering up beneath his lower eyelashes Then his eyes became senseless as an idiot's.

Dragonard lowered the dead man into the dark and rolled him over facing the dome's metal. False Regulators still crisscrossed the dim compound. The fight had lasted only a minute or so. By the grace of God or somebody, Dragonard had kept silence.

But he didn't know whether he'd make it now. His whole side ran bloody.

String the filament, policeman.

He fumbled with it. He stumbled up the stone stairs and waited until a Regulator pacing on duty at the top passed to the left. Dragonard lurched up and ran forward to the lip of the wall-walk and jumped.

He felt the filament twist hot and singing off the loop he'd strung onto his fingers. A man shouted and a blaster sizzled. Dragonard struck the earth. Pain and weird lights convulsed his insides.

"Deserter!" A man yelled on the ramparts. Another blaster burned near.

Blinking back sweat and pain, Dragonard raced

for the rocks. The filament unspooled from his hand, vibrating. He ignored the pain and pushed himself, working back into the high rocks. The filament spun out, snagging several times so that he had to double back to free it.

Everything turned into a slipping, stumbling nightmare. He felt he could go no further yet he pushed himself on. Rocks. Three moons. Hallooing voices behind— St. Anne had really gutted him.

Finally, a good mile from the perimeter of Kalrath, Dragonard found a small open place lit by the moons. He sank down on his belly and his blood soaked the rough earth. The almost invisibly thin filament disappeared around a rock back the way he'd come. On the rock itself a huge smear of his blood glistened like black enamel. He cradled the thumb-push in his hand and tugged on the filament.

Very little slack remained in it now. He'd undoubtedly snagged and snubbed it around a dozen rocks as he ran. Would they see it running up and over the wall? Had they found St. Anne yet? The odds in his favor seemed next to nonexistent.

Dragonard hitched himself around so that he faced Kalrath, though he could not see it because of the maze of intervening rocks.

If the filament remained intact it would be close to a minor miracle. He heard a confusion of shouting voices—they were searching for him. His breath whistled eerily in his ears. His whole belly and upper legs felt fluid from the leaking blood.

The longer he waited, the greater the chance

they'd discover the filament. Dragonard fought to hold onto consciousness. He crooked his thumb over toward the push.

On the flesh at the nape of his neck he felt the sudden prick of the tip of a knife.

XXIII

"LEAVE IT alone, Max. You aren't going to use that detonator. Max? Do you hear me?"

Dragonard risked no sudden movement. "Take that knife away."

"Put the detonator down first. Set it down away from you."

Slowly Dragonard moved his hand to the right. He held the thumb-push with thumb and forefinger, a miniature crane-jaw that gently lowered the bit of plastic to the earth. Then he drew his hand back.

The pressure of the knife vanished.

Dragonard rolled onto his back. He sat up and started to rise. The knife slid forward to touch his throat.

"Don't stand, Max," Jeremy said. "Sit. You can't jump me that way."

Through the rocks voices bawled orders, hallooing from the left and from the right. Jeremy had crept up past boulders behind him. His blue eyes glared; his hair and the ragged edges of his torn cloak flapped in the faint wind. He resembled a maniacal scarebird, the kind peasants staked into their field plots to frighten scavengers away.

Dragonard considered a quick move to disarm Jeremy. It would be difficult: Jeremy had a dagger and acted much more coherently than when Dragonard had seen him last. A hardness had settled onto his face, a rigidity that indicated his determination.

"How'd you get here?" Dragonard asked.

"I came to my senses back there." A hand waved toward the jumble of moonlit peaks running away to the south. "I realized you'd gone and must be up to something. Then I saw Neel. I remembered hearing talk about explosives. Neel was carrying them on his belt. I remembered that too. But he didn't have them any longer. I doubled back to find you. I've been searching ten minutes or so. Did you get that stringing the filament?" Jeremy's blade glowed as he pointed at Dragonard's bloody clothing.

Nodding, Dragonard said, "Jeremy, I think we can blow up Kalrath. The longer we wait and talk, the better the odds they'll find the filament and cut it. They're all over those rocks. I went inside the compound and they spotted me as I came out. You can hear them."

It was true. Now fading, now growing louder, syllables and phrases shouted by the search parties climbing up through the rocks came to the two men on the wind.

Jeremy blinked once. And again. Dragonard hurt from one end to the other.

"Blow up Kalrath?" Jeremy looked pitying. "You're crazy."

"It's the only way now, Jeremy."

"All my life, Max—all my life's gone into taking and holding Kalrath. It was the one lever we had to use on the Lords."

"But Mishubi has it now, God damn it! He's in there! He *controls* it!"

Uncertain, Jeremy brushed at his forehead. "We can take it back—"

"Not in a millenium. Not with what's left of the Heart Flag."

"The people have a right to the knowledge locked up in there—"

"Will they get it if we slink off and leave Mishubi in control? If we do that, he's won it all. His palace coups will solidify his position. We've got to blow the place up, Jeremy. Let Mishubi die."

Jeremy shook his head. "The knowledge inside Kalrath has been lost to people for too many years, Max. Lost too many years for us to wipe it out again. Once the organ banks are gone, there's no chance for people to be healed with what's stored down in the tunnels. This is the only place in II it exists. You know that."

Dragonard strained forward. He could practically hear the fall of the hand of some invisible clock, throwing away second after second . . . throwing away every chance they might have now . . . throwing away what he'd gotten this damn wound to arrange. He recognized Jeremy's blind spot and had a sinking feeling about arguing him around it. Still, he had to try.

"Do you think that if we blow up Kalrath, all the technology it represents dies?"

"Yes, what else? That's why I came to stop you, Max."

"It's not true. You're a simpleton if you think it is."

"I don't understand."

"All we destroy if we blow up Kalrath is Mishubi and his ambition. His coups won't work if he's dead."

"But the organ banks will be—"

"You can't destroy knowledge that already *exists!* If we blow up Kalrath we'll wreck Mishubi, all right. And the rule of the star kings you hate and I do too now. But with Kalrath gone we'll have a real chance. The chance to go from planet to planet, secretly and quietly but with plenty of time. And as we go we can tell the truth—the truth about repair of damaged bodies being possible. *Possible!* We've lived so long believing it couldn't be done, it's hard to see that the knowledge that it *can* be done is something altogether apart from the reality inside that fortress. If people know the renewal of life is possible, someone will rediscover the ways to bring it about. That's the real secret of the North Waste, Jeremy. Not the organ bank itself—just the fact that it exists."

Waiting, Dragonard watched for a reaction. He feared he'd confused Jeremy, who was hardly receptive in his present state to any kind of logical thinking. Jeremy's cheek went tic, tic. He held the dagger near Dragonard's throat and raised his free hand to still the facial spasm.

"You think all that matters, Max, is that people *know* they've been tricked for centuries?"

"Yes! With Mishubi dead and the organ banks gone, there'll be new freedom—"

"And some bright technologist somewhere will figure out how to synthesize parts?"

"Yes."

"How long will it take?"

"My God, how do I know. A century, maybe. Ten years. How can I answer that? But it's the only acceptable choice."

Jeremy's head lifted. He seemed to be staring over Dragonard's head and through the rocks at Kalrath. Voices grew louder to the left of them and boots scraped in shale less than half a mile away.

Jeremy's eyes brightened. Dragonard gripped his side but it wasn't possible to physically hold in the pain. He breathed in a shallow way, Jeremy frowned, thinking. God, if only his failure as a leader hadn't muddied his mind so!

Jeremy's shoulders lifted and fell. He turned his flaming blue eyes on Dragonard.

"No."

"What?"

"No, Max. You can't blow up Kalrath. I've given nearly all my life to take it. I've fought to hold it. I'll win it back. We'll win it back together."

Dragonard's gold eyes burned. "Count me out, Jeremy. There's just one way and it's my way."

"Don't force me—"

"Yes, I will. I'm going for the thumb-push and you'll have to kill me to stop me."

"I will." Tears ran out of Jeremy's eyes. "I will kill you, Max."

Dragonard lifted his right hand. He watched Jeremy with fixed intensity.

"Don't make me do it, Max."

"You don't understand what'll happen if Kalrath stands."

"I understand that everything I ever lived for is Kalrath, Kalrath itself, not the idea—"

"Then kill me, Jeremy, because I'm going to blow her if you don't."

Dragonard waited in the silence. He waited to spring. There would barely be seconds. Depending on Jeremy's reaction time, he might reach the thumb-push. Outlines of boulders, the peaks, the arching moons grew indistinct.

Jeremy sucked in a breath. He crouched with the light of the moons streaking silver on the flat of his dagger. Veins erupted into relief under the skin of Jeremy's hand as his fingers tightened up.

The final gamble, Dragonard thought with weary relief. *God, I'm exhausted.*

Tears ran down the dust on Jeremy's face. He rammed his knife hand forward. Dragonard rolled out of the way as fast as he could.

Jeremy's thrust missed and he sprawled onto his chest. Dragonard flung out his right hand but he was a few inches short of the thumb-push. Jeremy stumbled up. He raised his dagger over his head.

Dragonard tried to crawl forward but pain hindered him. His leaden fingers wouldn't stretch far enough.

Jeremy loomed against the moon-strung sky, mad, prophetic, his cloak flying.

Dragonard knew it was all over.

"Unnghh!"

The brutal cry of hurt burst out of Jeremy's mouth. He stiffened and rose on his tiptoes. The dagger fell from his hand. He slammed forward on his face, unmoving.

Up from his back just beneath the right shoulderblade struck another knife, pushed home to its hilt.

Bel knelt beside her brother. Dust covering her fighting-harness. The tunic beneath was nothing but a few fabric scraps held together by threads now. Her breasts thrust out half bare and heaving. Her dark red hair fell past her cheeks like streams of rain. Talking to both Jeremy and to Dragonard, she twisted and tugged at the dagger's hilt to free it.

"I followed him, Max. I saw him go and followed."

"Where have you been? Back in those rocks?"

"Yes. Waiting, listening. I— didn't know which of you was right. Not till I struck him. I didn't aim to kill him. I want him to live. I only wanted you to have your chance." She lifted her streaked cheeks. Dirt and tears mingled. "You're the right one this time."

Off among the rocks, voices of the pursuers shuttled back and forth:

"Yonder, yonder! I'm damn certain I heard a yell."

"Where's the rest of the patrol?"

"Converge, converge left, all of you! They're just up ahead–"

Quickly Dragonard examined Jeremy's wound.

"Deep, it looks like. But into the heavy muscle. He ought to live."

Bel brushed back her hair. "Can you walk if I drag him?"

"Yes. They're almost on us."

Bel began tugging at Jeremy's body, her hands in his armpits. Dragonard stumbled back toward the thumb-push. He picked it up. He thought about the filament strung out over such a long distance and then said to himself, *What the hell. It's too late to worry.*

Over went his thumb, and down hard on the stud.

Fortress Kalrath blew in a sheet of fire that climbed half a mile up the sky of Pentagon.

The dome will go in, crush down on the first tunnels, Dragonard thought as he turned to stagger after Bel. *And the weight of the first tunnels will crush the ones below.* He laughed. The pain seemed to lessen in his side.

He caromed off a rock. Startled yells from the pursuers changed to cries of terror. The pursuit ended abruptly as Mishubi's mercenaries went scampering back toward Kalrath to see what was left.

"Nothing," Dragonard said aloud. "Nothing left."

Bel saw his face, gold-eyed and awful. She shuddered and kept dragging Jeremy.

XXIV

Twenty-eight men of the Heart Flag survived the fight at Kalrath.

A day and a night later, they camped under a monument rock well outside the ring of electroguns. They'd had no difficulty slipping out through the ring this time.

Several of the men were severely wounded and heavily bandaged. The small band was composed about equally of fighters native to Pentagon and mercenaries. Two of the mercenaries had volunteered to remain with the Heart Flag and Dragonard had given the others leave to go. Grumbling, they were packing up to look for some other fighting job on some other world, one which offered them chance of payment for a change.

A herd of nearly fifty beasts had survived. One of the Pentagon men had ridden off with three and returned with rations kept in a cache a distance away from the mountain peaks. Over those peaks north of them, reddish light still flickered as the heat from the destruction of Kalrath slowly simmered out.

Jeremy still lay sleeping on an improvised litter.

His wound had been dressed with a few simple supplies from the desert cache.

Dragonard too had long thick yards of coarse cloth wrapped round and round his ribs under his tunic. The wound hurt fiercely. But an infernally bothersome itch indicated that the med dust Bel had sprinkled on the gored skin before she bound it was working.

They concluded their meal and mounted the beasts. The extra animals were strung out riderless in a long tether-line. The enormity and silence of the desert in moonlight frightened Dragonard tonight more than it ever had. The grumbling mercenaries rode off at full gallop into the east without so much as a glance backward.

Leaning forward in her saddle, Bel spoke to those who remained.

"We'll ride all the way through the Waste to Freeport Towne. It's smaller than Gannonblock, but not so well policed. We can rest there. I know people who will hide us. After that, we'll organize, determine assignments, decide who will go to which world. It will take a long time. We'll all have to take jobs first to earn passage money."

Dragonard sat listlessly in the saddle. His beast stamped and snorted, *chu-wuff,* anxious to be away. He wondered what had been the outcome of Mishubi II's palace revolutions now that the Lord himself, the prime mover, had died and left the rebels leaderless. He put the thought out of his mind. They'd learn in Freeport Towne, perhaps.

Bel continued speaking. Dragonard only heard

part of it. His gaze wandered to the range of low peaks up there past the electrogun perimeter. The redness danced and limned the mountains like the glow from the campfire they'd just kicked out.

Kristin. Kristin. He ached inside, thinking of her.

"—and it will not be easy, or quick," Bel continued. Her voice, though quiet, carried a new authority. Her red hair was held back with a headband made from a scrap of scarlet cloth she'd found somewhere. The ends of the cloth band fluttered out past the knot she'd tied, little scarlet flags. "Those of you who ride now will be committed, so those of you with doubts should go the other way, and no one will think less of you."

Bel paused.

No one moved.

A Pentagon man rubbed his flat nose and hunched over his beast's back. Another adjusted his sword scabbard on his hips. His fighting-rings tinkled on his arms.

"Good," Bel said. "This is the Heart Flag, then. Smaller than before but armed with a secret that one of these days can bring healing back to II. In time, with patience, we can spread the truth on the planets. We can make people know that long life is a birthright belonging to every man, not just the star kings. Now let's ride."

The Heart Flag men stirred. Two picked up Jeremy's litter and slung it between a pair of beasts with empty saddles. A rig of ropes suspended the litter and held it level. Traveling would be slow until Jeremy regained strength, but all of them had the rest of their lives to spend in the cause, and the North Waste should be free of Regulator harassment for a time.

Suddenly doubts went through Dragonard like spears.

This was foolish. He was a policeman, not an outlaw.

But of course he was no longer a policeman at all. He'd come too far and, like it or not, there was no returning. The Heart Flag had become as much his little army as anyone else's. He hadn't planned it that way, but there it was.

Well, men of the house of Dragonard had followed some strange paths in II Galaxy over the centuries. Let his sons and grandsons, if he ever had any, write whether Maxmillion Dragonard had been a savior or a lunatic. He gave up thinking about it and tightened his right hand around the rein. On his little finger the gold ring with the black stone and the twin emblems of the snarling lion and rising phoenix gleamed dark.

Bel jockeyed her beast up alongside his. She looked strong and quite beautiful.

"You're grieving for that girl," she said.

"I will, Bel, for a long time."

She didn't smile. She merely said, "When the grieving stops, Max, we'll still be together."

Dragonard saw her in a new light. Her body and bearing were proud despite the crudeness of her clothes. The scrap of scarlet tied in her wine-colored hair lent her an oddly girlish, frivolous air.

"Yes, I suppose we will be," he said.

For the first time he saw and understood the love in her eyes. He felt nothing but the ache for Kristin. Yet an admission of Bel's beauty came easily to mind.

He reached across and touched the back of her hand for a moment. She smiled.

Under the triple moons, the Heart Flag rode into the north toward Freeport Towne.